PASSIVE INVESTOR'S GUIDE TO REAL ESTATE PARTNERSHIPS

HOW TO EVALUATE APARTMENT BUILDINGS & MANAGING PARTNERS

FLEMING SCHUTRUMPF

AWARD WINNING AUTHOR

Printed in the United States of America
First Printing 2019
First Edition 2019
ISBN 978-1-7330474-0-1

10 9 8 7 6 5 4 3 2 1

TO MY SON ALARIC:

Who inspires me to do more and be more,

and,

who reminds me that love is a greater motivator

than all the money in the world.

Table of Contents

"High achievers are more afraid of not living their potential than they are of taking a risk and failing."

- Tony Robbins

"The secret to getting ahead is to get started."

- Mark Twain

"Don't wait. Life goes faster than you think."

- Paulo Coelho

"To reach your full potential, you need a team at your back that has the skills and passion for things that don't match your personal interest."

- Robert VonEschen

The Psychology of Winning

"People with the best lives have the best choices. People with the worst lives have the poorest, most limited set of choices."

- Tony Robbins

"Most people would assume my business success, and the wealth that comes with it, have brought me happiness. But I know I am successful, wealthy, and connected because I am happy."

- Richard Branson

All of us want to grow our income and increase the choices we have in our lives: choices to give more, be more, and do more of the things we want, for the people we love, at all the times we choose.

Investing in passive real estate partnerships (PREPs) can provide the means for those dreams to come true. We don't need to be real estate experts to be very profitable real estate investors.

The psychology of winning is simpler to describe than it is to live out. Yet all of the abundantly successful people I have met or studied live and embody this mindset at a deep level. The philosophy of success is independent from knowing the ins and outs of real estate, or of structuring passive real estate partnerships. Instead, the philosophy of winning is much more fundamental, which is why I cover the mindset of success first, before moving on to the mechanics of passive real estate partnerships.

Distilled most simply, the psychology of winning is as follows:

- **Set goals.** Without goals, we are just a cork bobbing on the ocean. Others, often bosses, friends and family, rope us into supporting the achievement of their goals and dreams while our desires, not fully written down and fleshed out in a way that can create positive momentum, are disowned or whither on the vine. "People with goals succeed because they know where they're going." - Earl Nightingale

- **Trust**. Believe and trust that you deserve the positive outcomes and that you have the wherewithal to attract the right partners, circumstances and possibilities to make your dreams come true. This is about knowing that we are worthy of success, regardless of any trash-talking we heard in our past about successful people being bad, dishonest and what not. We deserve to be successful people who can choose to use our successes to do good in the world. "You must trust and believe in people, or life becomes impossible." - Anton Chekhov

- **Face your fears with positive self-talk**. Cultivate the awareness that many of the things we fear are more threatening while galloping around in our heads than when we write them down on paper. Look at the likelihood of the fear truly coming to fruition, and simply make the contingency plans you can make to address that fear. In virtually all cases, if not all, you are more powerful than the feared scenario. You can overcome it, if it did somehow come to pass. "In many ways, life is about managing your delusions; keeping the ones that nourish and eliminating the ones that poison." - Steve Maraboli

- **Be present**. Cease ruminating on past missed opportunities, failures and regrets. However often you revisit the past, you will not encounter anything new. Instead focus on the here and now. Look at things you can positively influence now, and choose to have the most positive reaction you can muster to everything else. We cannot fully choose our circumstances, yet we have full control over our reactions. I personally find that the most beautiful people I encounter are not those who have been blessed with amazing circumstances, but instead those who encountered very challenging circumstances and chose an amazing response to them. "The good old days are now. Let's go make some money." - George Ross

• **Maintain a positive, optimistic outlook**. I have never met a winner, or any highly successful person, who was perpetually negative and agonizing over the negative outcomes that might occur. A trait of being successful is seeing the positive more than the negative. Many philosophies, from the Bible to the Law of Attraction, teach that what we focus on or believe is what comes to pass. Anytime we are tempted to engage in rumination, catastrophizing and negative self-talk, we greatly benefit from shifting our focus to positive aspects of our lives and staying as positive as we are able. The more we practice this, the more we live this as a habit that becomes our personality. Acquiring the habit of a positive outlook will drive further positive results and outcomes to further reinforce our positive outlook. "I really like my life. I've arranged my life so that I can do what I want." - Warren Buffett

• **Own your power**. We are all powerful, but not all of us have a practiced habit of acting that way in all dimensions of our life. Even when we don't admit it, we own our destiny. The thoughts we engage in translate into the actions that determine the quality of our lives. Therefore, we must realize that we owe it, not just to ourselves, but to everyone we love and care for, to own our actions and act in a way that puts the most abundance, prosperity and positive emotions into the world. As stated by Hillel: "If I don't act for me, who will, and if not now, when?"

Passive Income

"The moment you make passive income and portfolio income a part of your life, your life will change. Those words will become flesh."

- Robert Kiyosaki

"You become financially free when your passive income exceeds your expenses."

- T. Harv Eker

We don't need to create a day job out of our investment. Certainly, passive real estate partnerships will never require that from you. One of my early partners invested in a small multifamily building with me shortly before also purchasing a hair salon franchise. That franchise didn't deliver on its promises, even as our multifamily partnership did abundantly. Both he and his wife, at least on alternating days and sometimes both together, ended up commuting 80 miles round-trip daily, seven days a week to supervise the salon, instead of enjoying their retirement as they did previously. Otherwise, stylists wouldn't show up on time, and they wouldn't account for haircuts correctly—for instance, up-charging and pocketing the difference as a "tip" from the customer. The business in general would have continued to lose money, threatening the couple's very investment in the franchise, premises and equipment.

Real estate is different, if set up correctly, as in a good passive real estate partnership. It certainly is not "retail jail." Moreover, the managing partner is as motivated as you are to make significant returns for the partnership. There is no active management component for the passive partners. When the partner described above was forced to sell his share of our real estate partnership to infuse cash into his struggling hair franchise, he told me his passive real estate partnership with me had been the best investment he'd ever made.

Yes, real estate is a business where the property does require day-to-day management decisions and paperwork, yet this is managed by the managing partner. As a passive investor, your real estate income is passive.

What Is My Highest and Best Use?

"The hard part about following your purpose is the distraction everyone pulls you toward."

- Kimbal Musk

"Deciding what not to do is as important as deciding what to do."

- Steve Jobs

"Focus on what matters, ignore the rest."

- Stephen Covey

"Focus on signal over noise. Don't waste time on stuff that doesn't actually make things better."

- Elon Musk

We all have a day job, and myriad daily responsibilities which include everything from loading the dishwasher to picking our socks off the floor, to maybe even making sure all of those are laundered, dried, and neatly arranged in their respective places.

None of those activities has a lasting impact on the quality of our life in the way that deciding and acting to engage in a real estate investment can. The more we can prioritize our time on finding the investment opportunities that move us closer to our goals, the more we can focus on the real things that matter in life: **sharing time with those we love, and helping those we choose to offer our support to.** Yes, the toys and trinkets are fun for a while, but these other two things create lasting satisfaction and joy.

Why Real Estate?

"Landlords grow rich in their sleep without working, risking or economizing."

- John Stuart Mill, political economist

"Don't wait to buy real estate. Buy real estate and wait."

- Will Rogers, actor

"The best investment on Earth is earth."

- Louis Glickman, real estate investor and philanthropist

"Now, one thing I tell everyone is learn about real estate. Repeat after me: real estate provides the highest returns, the greatest values and the least risk."

- Armstrong Williams, TV host and commentator

When speaking with anyone who bought a house long ago, I see that this seemingly avoidable decision, they somehow proceeded with, changed their life more than anything else they did.

My sister's boyfriend's parents bought a house in the London, UK metropolitan area for about "around a hundred thousand quid" in the early 1970s. That loan got paid off over its repayment period. By 2016, the house was worth £11,000,000 (yes, that's eleven million British pounds, which is a lot of quid). In the UK, but also virtually everywhere else, there was a generation of people that became supremely wealthy through owning real estate in a location that is a desirable, high growth population center. It is up to us whether we choose to become the next generation to accomplish something like this.

Max, the repair man who adjusted my garage door in Denver, Colorado, had a similar tale. His parents bought a large Victorian property in the 1950s for $5,700. In 2015, his dad sold the house for $650,000. The purchaser did an extensive remodel, and the stately, fully-remodeled house in 2017 was estimated at being worth close to $1,000,000.

What About People Who Said "Just One Is Not Enough?"

"If you can do two or three or four, that's where wealth gets created."

- Mark V. Hurd, CEO of Oracle, HP, NCR

"Money isn't the most important thing in life, but it's reasonably close to oxygen on the 'gotta have it' scale."

- Zig Ziglar

Now you enter the arena of the people who have hacked the system. Governmental policies tend to be designed to allow ordinary citizens to own a single house so that they can have the security that makes them happy voters. Yet, the people who experience disproportionate economic returns are those who realize that one house isn't enough. If one property can increase in value more than 100 times, how about owning several?

Consider the case of somebody who bought 10 houses and instead of having a hundredfold increase in value, she or he actually got a thousand fold value (10 x 100 = 1000) compared to her neighbor who only owns one house. Of course, it took more investment. But, as one business professor told me, his house was *"essentially free."* Yes, he was being arrogant and looking backwards and comparing $3,000 back then to $3,000 now; we know they're not the same in terms of purchasing power and how easy they are to accumulate. Regardless, knowing that these trends have always held up, makes it foolish to not invest that next sum of money now on a growing investment. Looking back, that sum of money in 20 years, or much sooner, will seem like chicken change.

Taking the Plunge

"The biggest risk is not taking any risk."

- Mark Zuckerberg

"The people who are crazy enough to think they can change the world are the ones who do."

- Steve Jobs

There are investors who get into the market and take a position intended to create a return on their investment. Not all win, but the act of taking an investment position is required to come out winning. The people who really lose are those who remain outside the market, looking for that perfect opportunity that never quite comes along. They are excluded from any potential gains.

The perfect example of this is a family member. This is an uncle who drove me around Oakville, Ontario several years ago, showing me all the houses he could have bought since he got married in the mid-1970s. He could be a multi-millionaire by now. He clearly had the eye for real estate, but not the action. His story is filled with "shoulda's" and "woulda's," rather than with "I did". His bank account is emptier for it, and his lifestyle a lot less flexible. He doesn't get to choose how to spend his earnings; he is forced into budgeting. For him, in every decision he makes now, he has to consider financially driven tradeoffs.

Investing is a curious world. Taking a snapshot at any one point in time doesn't tell you the long-term reality. For example, an investor who bought a property in 2007 may have overpaid when the performance is looked at in 2008 or 2009. That exact scenario happened to me. I bought two homes in 2007 for around $50,000 each out of foreclosure. In 2009, an identical neighboring property sold for 30,000. However, in 2014 my property sold for $150,000. Did I lose? Sure, I could have won more. But, I never lost.

"I've been in real estate for my whole life, I've been trying to sharp shoot the market with my investments, I'm never right. All you need to do is get near the bottom. That's good enough."

- Barbara Corcoran

One of the world's great money managers is Dave Swensen. He grew the Yale University endowment from 1 billion to more than 20 billion dollars. Swensen says that market timing is an impossibility. What *is* completely possible is deciding to be in the market versus deciding to be out of it. The world is about controlling the actions we take that position us for success, and letting the rest take care of itself. We cannot control the market, but we can control that we are in the market in order to be able to benefit from it.

The real opportunity in investing is to create a team of individuals with complementary skills and assets. It's like the strategy Alexander the Great and his army used to create one of the most extensive empires of the ancient world, stretching from Greece to north-west India. Alexander did this by the time he was thirty years old, although he did start extremely young. He was undefeated in battle and is widely considered one of history's most successful military commanders. His secret weapon was the phalanx. A phalanx was formed of foot soldiers with interlocking shields and long lances that created a virtually impenetrable, tank-like fighting machine that could annihilate key portions of the enemy lines.

A phalanx cannot be created by one soldier, the same way that few of us can manage to be truly successful on our own. We require the spirit of teamwork and cooperation with aligned forces to be able to enjoy success in life and investing.

The passive real estate partnership is an example of how an alliance of warriors in the arena of real estate investment can achieve more than one can as a separate individual.

~ 10 ~

Trends Favoring Real Estate Investment More Than Ever

"Buy Land. They're not making it anymore."

- Mark Twain

"I'm a real estate guy."

- Robert Kiyosaki

"As income from work has become more concentrated in America, the super-rich have invested in businesses, real estate, art, and other assets. The income from these assets is now concentrating even faster than income from work."

- Robert Reich

Our world is in a state of amazing transformation. A larger percentage of the global population than ever before is living in cities, and by 2030, 60% of the world's population is expected to be living in cities.[1]

In 40 years, 2.7 billion more people will live in world cities than do now, according to the United Nations Department of Economic and Social Affairs. Urban growth in China, India, and most of the developing world will be massive. But what is less known is that population growth will also be enormous in the United States. The United States are the world's third most populous country, after China and India. It's not just about the size of our population. The US also has the highest population growth rate of the industrialized nations.

---

[1] https://blogs.worldbank.org/opendata/tale-many-cities-monitoring-worlds-urban-transformation

Further, according to the World Bank, "the U.S. population will grow 36 percent to 438 million in 2050 from 322 million today. At today's average of 2.58 persons per household, such growth would require 44.9 million new homes. However, American households are getting smaller. If one were to estimate 2.2 persons per household—the household size in Germany today and the likely U.S. size by 2050—the United States would need 74.3 million new homes, not including secondary vacation homes. This means that over the next 40 years, the United States will build more homes than all those existing today in the United Kingdom, France, and Canada combined.[2]

That is great news for real estate!

By global standards, U.S. real estate is a bargain. This is the stuff of headlines such as "Foreigners snap up record number of U.S. homes." Foreign buyers closed on $153 billion worth of U.S. residential properties for the 12 months ending in March, 2017. That marks a 49% jump from the previous year, according to the National Association of Realtors.[3]

"About 10% of foreign buyers paid more than $1 million, and 44% of sales were all-cash purchases . . . Overall, foreign buyers purchased 284,455 residential properties . . . This is up a significant 32% from 2016 and accounted for 10% of the dollar volume of existing home sales."[4] National Association of Realtors Chief Economist Lawrence Yun said the following about this increase: "While the strengthening of the U.S. dollar in relation to other currencies and steadfast home-price growth made buying a home more expensive in many areas, foreigners

---

[2] https://www.citylab.com/design/2013/04/coming-bold-transformation-american-city/5437/

[3] https://www.cnbc.com/2017/07/18/foreigners-snap-up-record-number-of-us-homes.html, accessed September 17, 2017.

[4] https://www.housingwire.com/articles/40710-foreign-investment-in-us-real-estate-surges-49, accessed September 17, 2017.

increasingly acted on their beliefs that the U.S. is a safe and secure place to live, work and invest."[5] Yun anticipates this trend continuing into the future.[6]

Not only is foreign investment in the U.S. a great boon to the U.S. economy, but there are few other appealing markets globally for international real estate investors to consider. "Across America house prices . . . are now at fair value compared with rents and incomes. But thanks largely to their big cities, housing appears to be more than 40% overvalued in Australia, Britain and Canada."[7]

One factor is the U.S. having a strong currency that remains a global standard. Another is a very effective government with a strong constitution that guarantees clear and enforceable rights to all who reside or own in the United States. A third factor is low rates of corruption, such that laws in the U.S. actually mean something!

For part of my childhood, I grew up in Cape Town, South Africa, and my parents converted a good amount of foreign currency to purchase the house I spent four years growing up in. When my parents sold that house, and we moved to the U.S., that money had become virtually worthless with the value of the South African Rand having plummeted during the period we lived in South Africa.

Further, the racial politics in apartheid era South Africa in the late 1980s were cause for some real concerns around personal safety. I remember that when I moved to South Africa as a ten year-old, the school buses I rode on had metal grates around the driver's windows to prevent projectiles like rocks and Molotov cocktails from disabling the bus and

---

[5] https://www.housingwire.com/articles/40710-foreign-investment-in-us-real-estate-surges-49, accessed September 17, 2017.

[6] https://www.inman.com/2017/07/18/chinese-and-canadians-are-top-foreign-investors-in-u-s-real-estate/, accessed September 17, 2017.

[7] https://www.economist.com/blogs/dailychart/2011/11/global-house-prices, accessed September 17, 2017.

risking the lives of school children in riots. By the time I moved away, all school bus windows were covered with thick, close-knit iron mesh. In South Africa, as we had already seen in similar countries like Rhodesia (now Zimbabwe) and Kenya, non-indigenous looking immigrants, even if they were 2nd and 3rd generation, were not being protected. Indeed, a 2017 Newsweek article focused on Zimbabwe President Robert Mugabe's statement that those who had killed white farmers during the "controversial land reform program in 2000 that saw squatters invade and seize hundreds of white-owned farms around the country" would never face prosecution.[8]

One of my school friends, the son of a pastor, was a displaced Rhodesian/Zimbabwean. One night, during heavy civil war gunfire in their neighborhood, his parents loaded the family station wagon with what few prized family heirlooms and critical possessions would fit. The older brother rode "shotgun"—with a real loaded shotgun at the ready, as they headed south for the South African border, to what, at the time, was safety. They left behind their home, their furnishings and the bulk of their possessions, but got to stay alive and start over in another country.

In terms of investing outside the U.S. today, Colombia is now being touted as a top place on the entire planet to invest in real estate. Property websites recommend buying now before prices rise in cities like Cali, Bogota and Medellin.[9] 20 years ago, Colombia was not considered even remotely safe for a foreigner except with a team of bodyguards. Even

---

[8] http://www.newsweek.com/zimbabwe-president-robert-mugabe-white-farmers-651326

[9] https://www.liveandinvestoverseas.com/real-estate/9-best-places-to-buy-real-estate-overseas-2017/, accessed September 17, 2017.

recently, the 2017 Travel and Tourism Competitiveness Report ranks Colombia as *the* most dangerous country in the world.[10]

Just one presidential election can change everything, for the better or the worse, and foreign investors typically aren't allowed to vote, even in countries where voting actually means something. As one well-traveled individual told me, in a significant number of countries where prices might be tempting for foreign investors to buy real estate, foreign owners are "one socialist president away from their properties being worthless or even confiscated."

In the U.S., we are extremely blessed to have political, economic and legislative stability that is virtually unheard of in many countries. Investing in U.S. real estate is one of the best investment bets in the world. This holds equally true for US citizens and residents, as it does for non-citizens and overseas investors in U.S. real estate.

Renting is Good for Renters, and Landlords are King in a Renter's Society

"If you rent, that's it. You don't have to pay any interest to anybody. You don't have to pay any maintenance costs to anybody. You don't have to worry about whether the boiler is going to break down. While if you own your own home, you have a hundred aggravations."

- Edmund Phelps, economist, won 2006 Nobel Memorial Prize in Economic Sciences

"Stupidity is when you have a Land Rover and a Land Cruiser and still have a Landlord. Wise up."

- Anonymous

"Landlords grow rich in their sleep."

---

[10] http://www.thisisinsider.com/dangerous-countries-2017-5, accessed September 17, 2017.

- John Stuart Mill

You and virtually everyone else reading this book has at one point or another lived in an apartment. I know I did while I was in college, after college, and later again in graduate school. Regardless of how we feel about the ongoing debate of whether it is better to own or rent, there are certain stages in life where it is better, if not unavoidable, to rent.

These pertain to most young adults starting up on their own, and a good segment of the elderly. The elderly often no longer need the hassle of direct home ownership and responsibility for maintenance, especially in an era where there are a number of contractors who prey on the elderly and charge fees for simple repairs that are far out of proportion to the actual cost of the repairs.

My 77-year-old dad was charged about five times the normal price for a simple job that took six months to complete by a contractor in Boulder, Colorado. This con man contractor claims he is best buddies with the chief building official. He threatened that the City of Boulder building department would make my dad's life hell when my dad tried to hold this contractor to his promises. Luckily, this appeared to be threat rather than truth. Nonetheless, the stress added to the financial costs, making this transaction very unsavory. Being a renter would have saved my dad a lot of trouble. Merely the cost of that one project was equivalent to a year's rent, without counting the stress.

In times of economic downturn, when home values drop off below the purchase price and even the mortgage balance, the pendulum swings even farther towards apartments. As with the 2008 recession, there will likely always be a segment of the population that stops seeing the value in continuing to make payments in temporarily undervalued housing. These people choose to walk away from their house and the associated loan payments. They go back to renting in an apartment complex where the extent of responsibilities is limited to paying rent, following house rules, and calling the property manager if anything breaks.

Even without a recession, renting can be quite attractive. "Between 2006 and 2014, the number of people in the United States who went from being homeowners to renters jumped nearly five percent, according to Trulia. That meant more people searching for a home or apartment to rent, leading to a 22 percent increase in average rent costs in the 50 biggest housing markets during that time."[11]

According to Harvard University, "the decade-long surge in rental demand is unprecedented. In mid-2015, 43 million families and individuals lived in rental housing, up nearly 9 million from 2005—the largest gain in any 10-year period on record. In addition, the share of all US households that rent rose from 31 percent to 37 percent, its highest level since the mid-1960s."[12]

This is fascinating, because as landlords we have strong applicants who still choose to be our customers, even though they could easily choose not to: "14% of big city renters can afford to buy, but choose not to do so."[13] What this means is that apartment buildings are an extremely recession-resistant investment. During times of poor economics, people will flee from the higher priced housing options and return to apartments.

Some people talk about Millennials creating a renters' society. That may be bad news for single family houses in the suburbs, or small towns in rural America. However, apartment owners in metropolitan areas are

---

[11] https://www.mysmartmove.com/SmartMove/blog/transunion-landlord-survey-summary.page, accessed September 22, 2017.

[12] http://www.jchs.harvard.edu/sites/jchs.harvard.edu/files/introduction_and_summary_from_americas_rental_housing_2015_web.pdf, accessed September 22, 2017.

[13] http://realtybiznews.com/14-of-big-city-renters-can-afford-to-buy-but-choose-not-to-do-so/98734727/, accessed September 22, 2017.

still king in a renter's society, especially in the hip urban areas where Millennials love to congregate.

Regardless of how our demographics continue to evolve, housing is always going to be a primary need for the United States population. This is irrespective of how our population shifts traditional patterns of commuting and work. We see a transition from work being in centralized office buildings towards employees working from anywhere with Wi-Fi and phone connections. Entire call centers are now distributed across whatever apartment the worker lives at, as long as it is reasonably quiet and has access to a good internet connection. Irrespective of shifts in office and work locations, there's always going to be a need for rental housing. Along with such housing comes the transfer of rent money. Landlords have the privilege of collecting those funds.

Where to Buy: Stay in the Major Urban Centers

I recommend only buying in major urban areas with a strong, diversified economic base. A coworker of mine had partnered with some friends to buy a 40 unit property in a small farming town in Northeastern Colorado. At some point, there was a renewed focus on immigration enforcement, and all the meatpacking plants concentrated in that town were raided by *la migra*, the U.S. immigration agency. As a consequence of the enforcement, four of the meatpacking plants that had previously been flagrantly violating employment laws and hiring undocumented immigrants ended up shutting down. The pool of renters in that town dried up like a spring puddle on a hot summer day. After several months of high vacancies, resulting in negative cash flows, my friend and her partners decided to sell the apartment building at a loss, even bringing money to closing to get out of a bad deal.

Over the long term, this town has grown significantly and is now luring new employers and legitimate industries and employers with attractive relocation packages, because of its low land costs and the like. This makes me wonder if it might have made sense to invest when nobody (including me) saw the value there. However, in the short run, in smaller markets, the impact on housing providers and employers of a newly enforced government policy or other economic change, can be much more significant than in a major metropolitan area.

A basic consideration for me as an investor is to have a pool of tenants that is not nearly as vulnerable to sudden events like those my friend experienced. My personal philosophy is to avoid that risk of loss by simply staying in the large urban areas where there is much less chance of a disproportionate impact of any one industry upon the economic health of the city as a whole. Furthermore, if there were a massive negative event impacting the entire metropolitan area, I would utilize my better management to compete aggressively against other landlords, keeping my units leased at their expense. In a smaller town, where an entire segment of the population can just move to a more economically welcoming area, that strategy is much more challenging to implement.

Solving Others' Problems at a Profit

"Business is all about solving people's problems—at a profit."

- Paul Marsden, British writer, businessman and former Member of Parliament

"The best plan is to profit by the folly of others."

- Pliny the Elder

Fundamentally, there is strong inherent value in apartments. However, a savvy manager of a passive real estate partnership knows how to identify and purchase undervalued real estate. This goes to the old adage of the biggest profits going to those who are adept at solving the biggest problems.

Problems to solve include:

- Out of line operating costs higher than standard for the type of building and location
- Low occupancy rates (high vacancies that remain unfilled)
- Below market rents

All of these are solvable!

To address high operating costs, it is not hard to challenge tax assessments, get lower insurance quotes, replace a faulty heating or cooling system rather than merely bandaging it frequently at higher costs, install insulation or energy efficient windows, or fix leaky toilets that can each cost up to $100 in monthly water bills.

Likewise, low occupancy rates can be addressed by getting rid of problem tenants, actively marketing for new tenants, renovating units and common areas, and generally making the apartment complex an attractive, well priced, desirable place to live for a demographic that pays rent on time and treats their units with care.

Below market rents are another fully addressable concern. When bringing rents up to normal, fair market levels, some long-term tenants may leave, necessitating repainting and re-carpeting of units, but that is part of the business of managing apartment buildings. Doing those upgrades might further increase rents above and beyond what one might otherwise raise rents to in an older apartment for an existing tenant. Sometimes below market rents are simply a product of deferred maintenance, resulting in poor curb appeal and uninviting common areas. Proactive upgrades and cosmetic face lifts do a lot to create a new image and ambiance that justifies far higher rents.

None of this is rocket science. There are a limited set of factors that create problems for owners looking to sell their investment property. Problem conditions can be a potential gold mine, as a motivated seller will sell at an advantageous price to the buyer who is willing to take on (and fix) the seller's challenges in exchange for a profit.

Different Types of Real Estate

There are many types of real estate investments, all of which can be engaged as a passive investment with the right partners. These range from single family houses to the apartment buildings that are the mainstay of this book, although many of the principles here apply more broadly to all forms of real estate. There are office buildings, trailer parks, self-storage facilities, and commercial real estate ranging from strip malls and retail shopping centers, to warehouses, manufacturing facilities, gas stations, hotels, amusement parks, golf courses, and the list goes on and on. All of these have commonalities that are inherent to real estate as an asset class. Yet, there are also differences that relate to the clientele and how the specific asset is handled in terms of being a business that requires some amount of management. If held in a passive real estate partnership, the day-to-day management with customer service, decisions and paperwork will be handled in some form by the managing partner and the management team one assembles.

Alternative Investments

"More Americans have money in a 401k than own a piece of real estate, and they're getting screwed with rampant fees every day that steal decades of retirement savings from them."

- Tony Robbins

"When Facts meet Opinions, Facts win every time."

- Tony Robbins

"If you're not going to put money in real estate, where else?"

- Tamir Sapir, Billionaire, 410th richest man in world

"Don't be buffaloed by experts and elites. Experts often possess more data than judgment. Elites can become so inbred that they produce hemophiliacs who bleed to death as soon as they are nicked by the real world."

- Colin Powell

Stocks

For me the stock market has been an investment arena I never did well in. And then, I wonder how my life would be now if I had. If my small investments had reaped 30% or 100% gains, would it have changed my life the way real estate did? I'd say no. Taxable 30% gains on $6,000 do nothing for me other than provide bragging rights at a neighbor's barbecue party.

Tax deferrable gains of $150,000 on real estate sale allowed me to turn one property into several and really impacted how I feel, how I think, and how I live my life as an investor, rather than a dabbler.

Early on, having gotten my first corporate job out of graduate school, I bought substantial stock in my employer, AMS (AMSY, now GIB). I had bought stock in the company as the stock declined from a peak in the early 2000s, expecting that the precipitous drop off in stock value would quickly recover, as this stock seemed to have predictable up-down-up trends that would make it perfect to buy on the down slope and sell on the up slope.

However, in the end it took more than 11 years for that firm stock value to regain its peak in January of 2000. I'm not the type of glutton for punishment who would endure 11 years of nail-biting, hoping and waiting, so I finally sold at a steep loss. There are enough better investments of my time, energy and money.

I also learned that being an employee at a firm gave me zero advantage with regards to investing in the firm that I worked for. In fact, at all-hands meetings we were told that the news we were just getting had already been released to "the street" (i.e. publicly announced to Wall Street), and often I found that reading the press releases online gave me far more information than we were told at the company meeting.

A few years later, just before the Enron meltdown, I consulted to a startup firm that was Enron competitor whose employees would have jumped ship to Enron and its stock option packages in a heartbeat. Just months later, I saw people at Enron lose all their retirement. At the same time, this start up lost funding and rapidly melted down. In fact, I had worked with the executive team of this firm to create a strategy road map with points of focus of strategic differentiation, revenue opportunities and corporate objectives. This was on a long sheet of wide brown paper with hundreds of post-it notes on it. Around the time of the Enron meltdown, I was very startled to see this valuable corporate artifact, which I had worked on for months with the CEO and executive team, wrapped around a sleeping homeless man as a sort of strategic blanket. Aspirations of a billion dollar market cap were now wrapped around an alcoholic sleeping off his intoxication in a downtown alley.

I had become friends with a kind Director whose office was near the printer I used, while consulting at a major Telecom provider. This mid-level manager chose to work six months more before entering retirement to make his then hefty retirement account just a "tiny bit bigger." His sacrifice cost him! His total retirement portfolio, mostly invested in previously high flying telecom stocks, dropped by more than 50% in those six months, from north of a million, to south of half of that. The Denver Post reported at the time, "amid a multibillion-dollar accounting fraud [Qwest] stock topped $60 a share before dropping to about $1 shortly after the end of Nacchio's five-year tenure in 2002."[14]

This was a heartbreaking reminder to me of how risky stocks are and how dangerous it is to rely on stocks for any sort of financial security, even (or especially) in the firms and sectors I worked in and was convinced I knew intimately.

When is the last time you heard of anybody's rent going up and down based on the latest oil price shock, the latest conflict somewhere across the world, the latest ouster of the CEO or the latest allegation of fraud regarding drug trials for a pharmaceutical company? When is the last time you heard someone wonder, "Oil prices went up Friday? I will now lower my offer on the house I'm looking to buy." Or, "There was a fraud indictment against a major real estate firm CEO on Tuesday. Now all real estate across the board is down 15%." In the stock exchanges, this kind of logic runs the market. Yet the same logic seems utterly crazy when applied to real estate.

Real estate is a lot more resilient to the daily news flashes that make stock prices fluctuate like a cheap helium balloon tied to the fence on a windy day. You might come out and find the balloon gone, yet the fence, and the real estate it sits on, will still be there, solid and tangible.

REITs

Real estate investment trusts (REITs) are managed portfolios of income producing real estate that are traded on the financial markets similar to a mutual fund. They provide liquidity like a mutual fund, yet the underlying asset is in real estate. Like the mutual fund industry, these funds tend to generate far lower returns than being an owner of real

---

[14] http://www.denverpost.com/2012/05/04/victims-of-qwest-securities-fraud-get-little-back/ accessed 9/11/17).

estate directly through a managed partnership. As in everything, there is a cost/benefit consideration. The cost is returns; the benefit is liquidity.

If you ask me, I will take returns over liquidity any day. I can't buy a Porsche with liquidity, yet I can buy one with returns.

One concern I have about REITs is that there are many layers of management and fees, which the lean organization style of actively managed real estate partnership that I run simply doesn't have and doesn't need, and can't even justify. Moreover, it's not just the levels of overhead. There is a real cost to government regulation. REITs, being publicly traded, are fully exposed to volumes of such regulation. For example, one of the requirements for an REIT is to have independent property appraisals at least bi-annually. A third-party commercial appraisal can cost anywhere from $2,000 to at least $10,000 for complex, nonstandard properties. Just this one requirement, which is one of many that have compliance costs, can take a bite out of investor returns.

Bonds

Bonds, traditionally touted as a safer investment for those who cannot absorb the volatility in stocks, also have their own volatility. If interest rates rise to above the face rate of the bond, the par or face value of the bond will fall below the stated value to give investors the increased rates they need.

For example, a $10,000 bond with a 5% coupon rate will sell for $10,000 if rates are 5%, but the price would be lower than $10,000 if rates were to go up to 6%, so that the difference between the coupon rate and the actual interest rate is provided to the investor through a discount in the purchase price. Pricing the bond lower allows the investor to get the 6% return, since the bond itself only pays 5% and the extra 1% has to be made available through a bond price reduction.

Bond yields must reflect both current interest rates and the expectation of future inflation, priced in through a discount rate. Since real estate rents go up with inflation and can be adjusted as appropriate as leases come up for renewal, the need to accurately forecast inflation for investors in real estate is much reduced.

Further, bonds are different than real estate in that as the rate of market returns grows, the bond face value would decrease, since the fixed bond returns being lower than market returns lowers the price of the bond. However, in real estate, both the cash flows and the value of the underlying asset can increase simultaneously. The sale value of the property can increase while the income stream from the property increases through rent hikes and other factors.

Interest Rate Effects on Traditional Investment Types

Interest rate changes also can dramatically affect stock and bond values. In capital markets, with very liquid investments, money is highly mobile. Money will migrate to the place of highest returns. If interest rates go up, the investing landscape changes, and money will typically flow out of stocks and bonds. Stock prices drop while the cost of borrowing for companies rises. Rising borrowing costs crimp corporate profitability and cast a dark shadow on stock prices. Bond prices drop as the fixed bond returns decline below what is achievable elsewhere in the market.

Real estate is far more resilient. Long term leases are a key stabilizer for real estate. Income is stable because leases don't change due to short-term changes in key trends, like oil prices, interest rates, or supply chain disruptions that can create lots of price volatility in the stock and bond markets.

Interestingly, too, there is a high rate of rent inflation in Colorado at a time when the official U.S. government inflation rate is quite low. Any investment that is tied to officially reported inflation statistics versus true market forces is likely to underperform.

The beauty of real estate in the vast majority of the U.S., where no rent controls exist, is that real estate prices and the lease income can move with the market. The US government has very costly motivation to minimize the officially stated inflation right and the Consumer Price Index (CPI). As on analyst who has studied this issue in detail concludes, "to get an idea of the sums of money involved, for every 1% of CPI underestimation the federal government saves $8.4 billion on social security payments alone . . . [This] provides . . . for covert debt management through CPI under-reporting."[15]

Real estate won't change significantly in value with moderate interest rate hikes. Leases will go up over time at the increase of interest rates, or faster, such that major price volatility in response to interest rate changes is not required for real estate to reflect changes in the economy and how they affect future earnings potential of the real estate.

The beauty of real estate is that, as owners, we have control over our investment in a way that a stock or bond investor cannot influence the company he bought shares from, or the issuer of the bond. As owners of real estate, we can increase rent rates, upgrade property condition, lower expenses and optimize other factors that can shape the return beyond simply having a purchase price and hoping for the best, which is what the dominant pattern is for stock and bond investing. Unfortunately, as a stock owner, painting the IBM headquarters simply will not improve the value of my IBM stock.

---

[15] http://www.zerohedge.com/news/2014-11-11/how-much-does-cpi-understate-inflation, accessed September 22, 2017.

So What Types of Investment Are Best for Me?

"90% of all millionaires become so through owning real estate."

- Andrew Carnegie

"Real estate is an imperishable asset, ever increasing in value. It is the most solid security that human ingenuity had devised. It is the basis of all security and about the only indestructible security."

- Russell Sage

"Doubt can motivate you, so don't be afraid of it. Confidence and doubt are at two ends of the scale, and you need both. They balance each other out."

- Barbra Streisand

This book is not about telling you what not to do. I would never say *not* to own stocks, or *not* to invest in any other investment. However, real estate is a classic investment category known to have made and preserved some of the greatest fortunes in history. Simultaneously, there is nothing wrong with diversification, and I recommend having money sprinkled across asset classes for risk reduction.

However, for most corporate employees, the only retirement investment option provided is stocks. There is a giant lobby that profits off of billions of dollars in annual fees and junk charges from your stock investments. This industry is actively lobbying to keep its revenue machinery as the only allowed investment option in virtually every single corporate, nonprofit, educational and government retirement plan. That status quo, in my view, is one-sided and wrong. It hurts America, in terms of making it more difficult for Americans to retire early or prosperously, limiting the future spending power of millions of prospective retirees.

The good news is that there are options like self-directed IRAs and Solo 401k plans that let you move retirement savings out of stocks and into real estate without penalties.

Not investing in real estate is, in my mind, a grievous mistake. Owning a house is not really an investment, since you are not generating income for yourself, although you are benefitting from the appreciation in real estate markets.

Consider: If you live in the same house from the age of a young adult to when you pass, you simply grew an asset for your children to inherit. You didn't actually generate cash returns that helped improve your quality of life and financial security. Hence, I really want to urge you to consider investment real estate that truly provides cash flows and financial returns.

One point is that diversification makes sense if you have a lot of assets to protect. If you have little money, you are better concentrating in a high growth sector and making your little grow into a lot. As the famed multimillionaire and philanthropist Andrew Carnegie wisely said, ""Don't put all your eggs in one basket" is all wrong. I tell you, "Put all your eggs in one basket, and then watch that basket." The great successes in life are made by concentration."

The Four Positive Financial Dynamics of Real Estate

"Buying real estate is not only the best way, the quickest way, the safest way, but the only way to become wealthy."

- Marshall Field, entrepreneur

Investment real estate property like an apartment building or strip mall really is an investment with not just one, but four separate categories of rewards:

1. There is the **appreciation** of the asset which is recaptured at sale. This is like buying a non-dividend stock, so that you pay money to buy in and later get more money out when you sell. In real estate, over time, that amount increases relatively predictably based on historical trends.

2. There is **cash flow** from the ongoing operations and rental income of the property. These cash flows can vary over time, because vacancies can affect income, and also because capital expenditures can temporarily increase expenses. Yet, property is priced based on the income it develops. Cash flows are a prime reason and objective for investing. Capital expenditures, if done correctly to increase perceived value to tenants, will increase cash flows.

3. There is **equity**. As financing on the property is paid back, additional equity is generated. To gain the highest returns on any investment property, a portion of the purchase price should be financed. Financing too large a percentage of the purchase price can create negative cash flows, which is not a healthy way to invest. However, buying a property for all cash, without borrowing at least part of the purchase price, limits how many additional properties can be purchased. Since the real estate appreciation rate typically outstrips the bank interest rate it is always advantageous to finance approximately 50-75% of the property acquisition cost in order to maximize returns. The principal component of each mortgage payment creates an equity buildup that over time can become substantial. Look at any amortization schedule to see how equity grows as successive mortgage payments are made.

4. **Tax savings**. Real estate building ownership creates positive tax impacts through depreciation. Depreciation allows you to deduct an expense against your income that actually is merely a theoretical expense for tax purposes. Really, depreciation is a fictional expense that reduces your real taxation. It's the only fictional thing you can proudly point to on your tax return, where everyone, even the IRS, will nod their head and agree that the fictional concept is valid. Depreciation is permitted

only on items like buildings, which tend to age and lose value over time. Land is non-depreciable.

A good way to view depreciation is that we are allowed to get our original capital investment in the property back over time. When you invested cash in your building, and you now get that cash back, you should not be taxed on the return of your investment to you. Even as you get annual rental income, you deduct depreciation from that rental income and keep that deduction tax free to recover your original investment. Over time, the total of the depreciation you are allowed to deduct equals the original cost of the building.

But, Uncle Sam has a way of getting you back. When you sell the building, the depreciation will be recaptured and the tax benefit received over the years of rental will be paid back to the IRS through capital gains tax. However, this is still a benefit to you. Capital gains tax at 15% to 20% will typically be lower than your ordinary tax rate.

Why Is This the First Time I've Heard of Passive Real Estate Partnerships?

We see financial investment advice every day on TV, and in every magazine that has some hint of financial component to it. We receive "winning" stock-picking advice written by journalists who are, and remain, broke. I have yet to read of a recent journalist who followed the advice they gave others and then went forth to achieve such success that they became a true authority on wealth creation.

The Chief Financial Officer at my last corporate job was not much wealthier than the journalists whose drivel he subscribed to. Here was a self-proclaimed expert in high finance, with an MBA from Duke University to match. He subscribed to the whole lot of financial periodicals—everything from *Money*, to *Worth*, to *Smart Money*, as if the first magazine came from the dumb side of the family. Nonetheless, my best guess is that his lifetime achievement of net worth was limited enough that it could have fit in the equity of two or three of my rental properties, of which I owned 35 at the time. He left older copies of these financial magazines in the lunchroom, and I sometimes perused them while eating lunch.

It is amazing the drivel that is peddled by these financial periodicals upon normal Americans and Canadians looking to provide a comfortable retirement and a better financial future for themselves. The investment products written about in what should be journalism often read like thinly veiled advertorials. Most of these products appear to have layers and layers of overhead and management skimming at the very trough of returns that should by right go to the investors.

It's hard to be surprised. Being featured in a high circulation periodical often comes at a price. A reliable way to pay those advertising and publicity fees is to skim off investors' returns. Passive real estate partnerships, like those I assemble for the people I invest with, are different; my partners and I are direct owners of an asset for which we strive to maximize returns over the long run, without allowing anyone else to feed at the trough of our returns.

In the type of passive real estate partnerships I like to put together, management is lean, focused and efficient. We carefully scrutinize the financial reports submitted to me by property management. We strategize how to maximize long-term occupancy levels and resident satisfaction levels with targeted investments in capital improvements. Most importantly, we consistently focus on generating the best possible cash flow returns, while also maximizing resale value for a great exit strategy.

Flip vs. Hold

Both flips and holds of apartment buildings can have interesting returns. However, my belief is that long-term thinking and a long time horizon separate the true professionals from the dabblers.

Here is one property I offered on that I ended up not winning in 2010, that ended up changing hands several times in relatively short succession. This is 3485 West 68th Avenue, Westminster, Colorado.[16]

Date of Sale	Sale Amount	Seller	Buyer
03/02/1992	$0		
12/28/2000	$450k	ACIERNO PATRICIA L	WOLF EDMUND C
12/28/2001	$740k	WOLF EDMUND C	RAMIREZ RAYMUNDO AND
11/10/2005	$0	RAMIREZ RAYMUNDO AND	GUZMAN GLORIA
04/01/2010	$0	GUZMAN GLORIA	CRP PROPERTIES INC
09/24/2010	$325k	CRP PROPERTIES INC	R INVESTMENTS RLLP
03/25/2011	$720k	R INVESTMENTS RLLP	STANBERRY HARRIS I LLC
10/01/2012	$910k	STANBERRY HARRIS I LLC	CAPITAL 8 WEST 68TH AVENUE LLC
06/06/2014	$1.2M	CAPITAL 8 WEST 68TH AVENUE LLC	RELDAN REALTY CORP

---

[16] http://gisapp.adcogov.org/quicksearch/doreport.aspx?pid=0182505200064, accessed November 5, 2017.

My strategy of a long, 5 to 7 year hold would have gained all of the returns and increases in value that were allocated across a number of transitional owners, all of whom lacked long term vision. The opportunity started with a foreclosure sale for $325,000 that I bid on in 2010 (I actually bid more than the recorded sale amount, yet, to my lasting annoyance my offer was not chosen as the winning offer) and then culminated in a sale just short of three years later for $865,000 more. Yet that $856,000 in gains was distributed across three short-time owners, rather than a single entity having the vision and staying power to own an apartment building for 3 short years and really create serious returns.

Why make fast, small bucks on a rental property? Tenants pay the rent every month, so that the property creates cash flows. There is no need to get out and sell, when there clearly is further upside on the horizon, coupled with positive cash flows right now. The real returns are not made by people doing a quick dabble. The real returns come to this with commitment, staying power, and most of all, vision.

Sweat Equity

"Some people look for a beautiful place. Others make a place beautiful."

- Hazrat Inayat Khan

Sweat equity refers to buying a distressed property at a discount and then fixing the property up for less cost than the value being created. The equity is the difference between the fix up costs and the much larger value being created by the improvements. This is a wonderful strategy for the right property.

The best properties need lots of cosmetic work and very little in terms of serious upgrades. This allows for good estimation of fix up costs, and low risk fix ups create bigger predictability in terms of costs. At the same time, for the experienced investor or managing partner, the highest risk fixes are those that sell at the steepest discounts, since even other experienced investors may be hesitant to take on such a project. This is where the real gold mines can be, but only for seriously experienced and committed investors who are willing to take on the project most others will run from—and negotiate a commensurately low purchase price.

Financial Analysis: How Apartment Buildings Are Valued

"It's not what you make, it's what you keep."

- Julian Block, author and tax attorney

"Always focus on the front windshield and not the rearview mirror."

- Colin Powell

Cap Rates

In real estate, the cap (capitalization) rate is equivalent to the PE (price earnings) ratio for stocks. A real estate cap rate is simply the net operating income divided by the price. A stock PE ratio is the price per share divided by income per share. As such, the PE ratio is the inverse of the cap rate, and the cap rate has price in the denominator not the numerator. Typical apartment cap rates are in the range of 6-10%. Typical stock PE ratios are 20-25, which if inverted (1/20 or 1/25) for comparison to cap rates come out to 4-5%. Besides being more favorable, real estate cap rates are quite stable, while stock PE ratios often fluctuate widely. As an investor, I like the fact that regardless of the latest crisis, or even multiple crises screaming off the front pages of the newspapers, real estate cap rates are very stable.

The best way to look at cap rates is to simply see them as a metric for comparing competing investment options at the time of purchase. Three different properties might have three different cap rates, and each cap rate is a valuable data point in the analysis of an investment option.

Cash on Cash Returns

Cash on cash return is simply another variation on the payback metric. The cash on cash return measures the annual net operating income as a percentage of total cash invested. For example, the apartment building above, purchased for $1,000,000 all cash with a $70,000 annual operating income, has a 7% cash on cash return. The cash on cash return is a good, back-of-the-envelope means of comparing returns across different properties being considered for acquisition. Cash on cash returns vary based on the financing chosen. For example, the 7% cash on cash was an all-cash deal. If that same building had been purchased with a 70% loan, and 30% cash down payment of $300,000, the cash on cash return would have been 23% ($70,000/$300,000). Cap rates simply don't consider financing implications.

Payback Period

The payback period is quite simply the amount of time the operating income would take to pay back the entire purchase price. The payback period is an interesting number for comparison. The lower the payback period, the more attractive an investment opportunity is. It is often startling how relatively quickly cash flows from an apartment building will pay for the entire purchase price.

For instance, a property that cost $1,000,000 might have gross rents of $120,000 per year and a net operating income of $70,000 per year. That property would take 14 ¼ years to repay the purchase price at current rents if purchased using all cash. Raising rents over time will shorten that ratio. The main factor for many of these financial metrics is to compare different investment options as they perform in the year of acquisition. The payback period should get shorter as you own and improve the property. Based on the known factors in the year of acquisition, you can construct a sense of which investments look better than others.

Fundamentally, this is a measure of cash flow that tells you when the building has essentially become a free investment to you. I love the fact that a building gets more valuable, and throws off more operating cash, once you have reached the point where the property became free, just through normal appreciation and rent inflation over time.

Once again, this is a telling reminder of the benefits of thinking long-term. Those who buy and sell quickly reap small rewards. The real rewards are when the "golden goose" has returned all the cash you used to buy her, and is now laying bigger and bigger eggs. Smart investors who engineer their financial lives to not "need cash urgently now" reap returns over time that enable them to *never* "need cash urgently now."

Debt Service Coverage Ratio

At its heart, this ratio measures how property cash flows compare to the loan payments. The debt service coverage ratio (DSCR) or debt service ratio (DSR) is a variable lenders look at closely, since it is a measure of the security of the loan they might be considering extending to you. Essentially, the lender looks at the "net operating income" of the property, which is the annualized gross revenues less operating expenses, to see whether it exceeds the loan payments. Lenders typically look for 1.2 times the loan payments in operating income. As a savvy managing partner, I like it to be higher, at the very least 1.3, and ideally at 1.6 or higher.

To give an example, if the $1,000,000 building in the prior example has a net operating income of $70,000 and an annual debt service of $58,333, that creates a 1.2 DSCR. Then again, a higher ratio (meaning more operating income or lower debt service) is healthier.

For example, a 1.4 DSCR would require higher income of $81,666 against the $58,333 loan payments.

Economic Cycles

"People think they can handle risk, until they lose money."

- Tony Robbins

"Real estate goes up and down, upwardly."

- Raymond Aaron, speaker, author, real estate investor

Today's Bust Is Still Higher Than the Boom a Few Years Back

"The peak value in any given cycle has always exceeded the peak value in the previous cycle. So there was no question in my mind—even during the depths of the downturn—that we would get back to peak [price levels] because we always have. It's only a question of how long it takes to get there."

- James F. Peltz[17]

For the true long-term investor, the current value of your property is not of primary importance. History has shown us that even when property values decline, rents remain relatively stable. That means that even as sales prices of investment real estate can show cyclicality, rents are much less affected. Rents have long-term contracts (leases in place).

The costs and hassles of moving discourage tenants from finding a new property simply to save a few dollars each month. Finally, in a down economy, growing numbers of disgruntled homeowners revert back to being renters, swelling the pool of tenants looking for a rental even as their former residences may go through the drawn-out processes of

---

[17] http://www.latimes.com/business/la-fi-qa-home-prices-20160713-snap-story.html, accessed November 5, 2017.

foreclosure, becoming bank owned, and/or being listed for sale. Speculative purchases of houses for quick resale can be risky, since house prices can shift. However, rents historically remain stable even as other market indicators fluctuate. Lease contracts set lease rates for typically at least a year, further limiting volatility.

Financing

This is the evaluation of the benefits and tradeoffs of choosing to buy a property with cash versus financing a portion of it. There is a risk and reward trade-off. Buying all cash lowers the risk associated with making periodic loan payments. However, in many cases, buying with a loan can also lower your risk. A lender will perform due diligence that, though intended to protect them from lending on an asset that might not justify its repayment, also protects you by helping ensure that your investment in the asset makes sense. In terms of returns, it's easy to see that especially in the long-term, being able to buy two properties with financing is better for rent cash flows and underlying asset values than buying only one using all cash.

The easiest way to illustrate the power of borrowing to create greater returns is to show the following sample scenarios:

1.   In this scenario, we buy an apartment building for $5,000,000, all cash. The annual net income is $500,000. The total return is 10% ($500,000/$5,000,000). The four year return is 40%. (That's 4 × 10%, assuming no rent hikes for simplicity's sake for just this example. In reality, returns would be higher from factoring in the compounding effect of rent hikes.)

2.   In the second scenario, we buy that same apartment building for $2,000,000 in cash and $3,000,000 through financing. The net income is still $500,000. The $3,000,000 financing requires $200,000 per year in debt service. This is a 4.5% loan with a 25 year amortization and monthly payments of $16,674.97, which is annual mortgage payments of $200,100. We'll use $200,000 for simplicity. The net income is $300,000, and the partnership return is 15% (300,000/2,000,000) over

four years. Again this assumes no rent hikes for simplicity's sake, since we are looking at the effect of financing, not the financial effect of the compounding of rent hikes. This way your return is 60% (4 × 15%).

If you take scenario two and use the other $3,000,000 to make additional investments with the same returns illustrated in the first scenario, you will have made 5% more in scenario two, plus 15% on the other $3,000,000, so an extra $250,000 per year on your money versus just having bought that one property all cash. (You will have made $300,000 + $300,000 + $150,000 = $750,000 versus just having made $500,000.) Extrapolate that over four years, and you will have made an extra $1,000,000 (4 × $750,000 = $3,000,000 while 4 × $500,000 = $2,000,000).

That extra $1,000,000 in four years is the power of using financing versus all cash. In the first year, the difference may not seem that noticeable. But after four years, the variance grows substantially. This extra million makes a significant difference that can change what you are able to do with your time and your money.

Take an additional element of your total return that applies here, mortgage payback. Making the loan payments over the same four years will further increase your returns, as it creates just north of an additional $712,000 in principal payback that is additional equity across the sum of leveraged investments. Your total return goes to 74% over the four years.

Compare this to the 40% return with an all cash purchase, and the investor who financed part of the purchase price in the scenario here just outperformed the all cash purchase investment strategy by 85%. The return increases over time, and four years is a fairly short time horizon. Over time, the returns and the gap between all cash and leveraged investments can become even more massive. This is a strong argument for making a safe level of leveraged investment!

Please note that this is an illustrative example and that finding and managing properties to achieve similar real life returns takes an experienced syndicator, hard work, lots of due diligence and savvy management, and waiting the four years for these returns to develop.

The table below shows the two scenarios in tabular form:

			Net Income				Total at Year 4
	Investment	Loan	Year 1	Year 2	Year 3	Year 4	
All Cash	$5M	$0	$500k	$500k	$500k	$500k	$2M
Scenario 2							
Loans	$2M	$3M	$300k	$300k	$300k	$300k	$1.2M
	$2M	$3M	$300k	$300k	$300k	$300k	$1.2M
	$1M	$1.5M	$150k	$150k	$150k	$150k	$600k
Total with Loans	$5M	$7.5M	$750k	$750k	$750k	$750k	$3M
Principal Repayment			$166k	$174k	$182k	$190k	$712K
Total with Loans	$5M	$7.5M	$916k	$924K	$932K	$940K	$3.7M

If you are a parent with children who will eventually go to college, you may be feeling some tuition trauma. Even at tomorrow's inflated costs for college, the possibility of something like an 85% return on your money over just four years can dramatically lower your stress levels about giving your children access to the education, and the associated credentials, that are critical to their future economic success.

There are other considerations other than merely returns. Certainly there is less risk if there is no debt. However, the measure of a smart investing strategy is to balance a rough range of optimal risk and return, such that smart risk is balanced with positive returns to maximize return on investment to the partners.

"Opportunities will come and go, but if you do nothing about them, so will you."

- Richie Norton

"For example, if I make money, I put it in real estate. I always did very well."

- Ivana Trump

"Billionaires get in trouble when they don't watch their cash flow."

- Tony Robbins

Is a Passive Real Estate Partnership a Good Fit for You?

Who Should Invest in Real Estate Partnerships?

If you're just getting started as an investor and have a very small capital stake of less than $10,000, I would recommend staying away from passive real estate partnerships. For a real estate partnership to be able to buy an asset of adequate size to create the returns we are looking for, I recommend that partners have at least $25,000 to $50,000 invest, and ideally $100,000 or more.

If you have just $25,000, or whatever the amount of your nest egg is, and you invest that entire sum into the real estate partnership, you might no longer have a cushion available if other things come up. This is not something I would recommend.

Further. if you are over the age of eighty or so, unless you are an accredited investor with a net worth over a $1,000,000 and looking to diversify, I do not recommend a passive real estate partnership.

If you are a somewhat knowledgeable investor with a decent pool of money to invest, passive real estate partnerships should really be top-of-mind for you. You do not have to have real estate investing experience in order to successfully have excellent returns in a passive real estate partnership.

Being a passive real estate partnership investor is not primarily about having in-depth real estate knowledge. Having the right mindset is far more important. Mindset trumps knowledge any day. There are many people who work in the real estate field, who know the domain inside out, and who still make very little money. Only those who have the mindset of seeking opportunities, actively investing in the face of uncertainty and being willing to put in effort and take risks, actually gain the returns that separate the successful from the knowledgeable.

11 Steps You Can Take to Create an Investor Mindset:

1.   Formulate a burning desire for success. Determine what a successful investment can achieve and do for you. Whether you are motivated by a family you want to take better care of, a corporate day job you hate, the need to support yourself after a divorce, or your desire to retire comfortably, aim high and clearly visualize what success will look like for you. Take your dreams of becoming a successful investor seriously, and act. Take the decisive action that allows your dreams to become reality. Invariably, the successful investors who achieved the returns that upgraded their lives started with a fervent desire to achieve greatness and a willingness to do what it takes to get there.

2.   Successful investors are willing to make short-term sacrifices for long-term results. In other words, investors have the ability to prioritize investing over spending. My maxim was always that I would rather live like a college student a few years longer now, than live like a college student in my retirement. The power of compounding rewards early action, not remedial action late in the game. Nonetheless, late action is substantially better than never acting. Whatever age we are now (or in 5 years), we always get to look back and say, "I wish I had done that 5 years ago."

3.   Do not allow fear to hold you back. Instead of focusing on what could go wrong, focus on the opportunities, and on what could go right for you.

4.   Don't let *analysis paralysis* stop you. Making your first investment perfect is not a realistic expectation. There are people who research real estate investment options endlessly, and ultimately become overwhelmed with all the decisions. Remember, you're building experience by taking action on your first investment. The willingness to take action is just as important as the investment itself. What you really need to do is act—to take that first step.

5.   Acknowledge that mistakes and setbacks are part of any path, even the path of a successful investor. Look at every investment, regardless of the outcome, as a learning experience. Often we can learn more from a single failure than from ten successes. Keep matters in perspective, stay positive, and keep going even when things don't immediately or always look rosy.

6.   Buy on the numbers, not emotion. Review the returns on each potential investment. Be prepared to walk away if the numbers don't make sense. Also, be very prepared to actually move forward if the numbers are right.

7.   Many investors stop after one good investment and rest on their laurels. However, those with an investor mindset are aware of the compounding benefits of building a portfolio, reinvesting gains from one passive real estate partnership into the next in order to reap further gains in additional investment opportunities.

8.   Set aside time each week to focus on your property investing activities. View property investment as an exciting activity that you prioritize like an exciting hobby or an important relationship. Have exciting goals that keep you motivated. Periodically assess your progress to make sure you're on track to achieving those goals. Ideally, this might not

feel like work, but rather like paid play. It could be your high stakes adaption of fantasy football.

9.   Study and emulate successful investors. You may find they view investing as a way of life. Even the giants in their field continue learning and looking for new insights to optimize their skillset.

10.   Associate with positive people. There are haters and these are easy to spot and avoid. The bigger risk can be people who love you so much that they don't want you to get hurt. These well-meaning individuals may try to discourage or criticize your investment choices. Even when they are well-intentioned, don't allow anyone else to influence you to give up your dreams. Associate with people who are on the same path, and who share similar goals, for the support you need to stay the course.

11.   The partners I've had in the past frequently had little or no experience in investing in real estate. Often, they have had little interest in learning, nor did they need to. Because they have solid, detailed portrayals of their investment and of the property performance through the quarterly reports I provide, the majority of my partners do not show interest in touring the property or checking on its interior or its tenants. That option is certainly something that can be made available. Most partners, however, are interested in the financial returns, and they have direct access to me via phone and email or, depending on their location, personal meetings to address any specific questions.

There is no reason that an investor looking to build substantial wealth faster cannot be a co-owner of a 50 unit apartment property, a shopping center, or an office building, even though the financial media doesn't even present this an option.

I'm all about the wealth building benefits these kind of properties offer without the need for my investor partners to actively deal with the day-to-day operations.

Know Thyself: Are You Fit to Be a Passive Real Estate Partnership Investor?

"To know thyself is the beginning of wisdom."

- Socrates

"Life is like a game of chess. To win you have to make a move."

- Allan Rufus, author

A key component of knowing if something like this is right for you is to know yourself. Know if you can handle the uncertainty, and the inevitable ups and downs, that will occur in any real estate holding over time, whether held in a partnership or individually.

From a hindsight perspective, any deal that made a good return seems like a good deal. Yet, when looking forward without that certainty, the decision has to be one that you make. That decision must be one you can be comfortable with. In the end, risk tolerance is a key criterion in making money. If that is not your strong suit, there are other investment options that might have lower returns, but that also better match your personality style.

Ultimately, we are all descended from a long line of ancestors who braved the odds. They survived crises, wild animals and pandemics, as well as exploitative nobility and oppressive governments. Our ancestors did what it took to provide for themselves and their loved ones and to continue their bloodline. Staying poor in order to have a sense of certainty is not in our human DNA, no matter how much our educational system may have discouraged risk taking and had us abandon our inner warrior queen or warrior king.

Our time here on this beautiful planet is limited, and our job is to live in joy and help others live in joy. A successful real estate partnership can contribute to that. If we do not believe that a particular real estate partnership investing opportunity would contribute to that, or we don't see ourselves enjoying the process, we should honor that and seek a different passive real estate partnership, or other ways of investing our money.

Considerations for investing in any given passive real estate partnership opportunity include the following:

- Your income and cash flow outside the sphere of the passive real estate partnership you are considering.

- The predictability of your income outside the passive real estate partnership.

- Your liquidity: the amount of funds you have available to invest, and the amount of funds you would have remaining after investing in a passive real estate partnership to still handle any kind of emergencies that might come up, that might range from a failed transmission to a child or family member needing financial help.

- Your risk threshold: your comfort level in investing money. This is also your ability to wait and see, and soothe yourself through times of uncertainty and the potential down cycles your property may have.

The founding father of positive psychology, Martin Seligman, warns us against the folly of believing negative events to be *permanent, personal,* or *pervasive.*[18]

---

[18] Seligman, Martin E.P. (1991). Learned Optimism: How to Change Your Mind and Your Life. New York, NY: Pocket Books.

Why You Want and Need an Active Partner

If you don't know how to successfully invest in real estate, it only makes sense to partner with someone who does. At some level, it's like a person, who doesn't even know how to change a tire, either trying to fix their car themselves (not recommended), or taking their car to a random mechanic, who may or may not be skilled, fair and honest. Without knowing all the questions he needs to ask, and without some sort of relationship to ensure he is getting a fair deal, he is not positioned to get the best deal on the maintenance for his car, nor even possibly the most proactive maintenance on his car.

If the mechanic forgets to suggest something that should have been looked at and the part fails in a way that impact other components, like a timing belt breaking and destroying the engine, it's the hapless car owner who is responsible for the repairs, not the mechanic.

When passive real estate partnership investors partner with me, it's a bit like hiring a trained mechanic with extensive management experience and an MBA to deal with the other mechanics, the parts store, the recycling of old oil and tires, and all the environment laws and regulations—but there's much more. I manage the interactions with contractors, property managers, banks, local code enforcement and tenants, and then there are all the other various disciplines that are hard won skills I've honed over 20 years of doing this. I've made the rookie mistakes and learned my lessons the hard way on my own properties. You neither have to repeat those same mistakes I made (and that many beginning real estate investors fall into) nor partner with others who might be at risk of making those mistakes at your expense.

Evaluating and Selecting Partners

"The Way to Wealth is to do more for others."

- Tony Robbins

"If I hadn't been fair, I would never have made the $6 billion in real estate deals that I did. I mean, if you're not fair, people don't want to deal with you."

- Jerry Reinsdorf

Checking out a Prospective Managing Partner

It's worth checking that you have a partner who can deliver what they promise. Key criteria for a good partnership manager are business and management experience, real estate experience, property management experience and construction experience.

I share what follows as a basis for comparison of what a good managing partner resume might look like.

I started off after getting my MBA working for an IT consulting firm as a project manager and program manager, managing teams ranging in size from four people to up to 35, which in the latter case was seven people onshore in the US and 28 people offshore in China.

I've owned real estate since I was 21 years old, and I first got my real estate license in 2001.

I also got my general contractor's license in 2007 and have personally managed and substantially worked on more than 50 properties, running major construction and remodel projects.

I managed four different property management organizations and have seen the best practices that I use both in management in general and in property management specifically. Moreover, I also managed all of my first 35 or so rentals myself for a span of time. I fully understand the amount of time, effort and maintenance a typical rental property requires. This is critical, as some less savory property management organizations can look to boost their income by seemingly fabricating invoices for services that weren't needed, or actually weren't performed.

I've sold a very small percentage of my portfolio, but still a decent number, and I'm a licensed real estate agent familiar with the psychology and activities required to successfully buy and sell various types of real estate.

It is no longer a good use of my time to do many of the day-to-day property management details myself, but I have done them for a long time and I understand the intricacies involved, the questions to ask and how to make sure everything is on the up-and-up. This is the same as a mechanic taking his own car to a different mechanic when he is too busy to fix the car on his own, or dentist going to another excellent dentist for his own dental care. He knows what questions to ask, and the amount he gets charged is going to be much lower than the average automobile owner with limited car knowledge taking their vehicle to any random mechanic with few selection criteria other than proximity, and convenience.

Partnerships are both easy and complex. The easy part is to define as many likely scenarios upfront, and then let trust and good working relationships between the partners take care of whatever else might come up.

Business partnerships aren't that far off from a romantic relationship. Money can be almost as intoxicating as love, and it can be just as overloaded with beliefs, hopes, misgivings and fears. Like in love, a business relationship benefits from a clear set of expectations for how to act and respond in defined situations, and a framework for managing communications. This allows us to much better enjoy the ride with an investment property and the partners we have chosen.

The challenge is in anticipating possibilities that cannot be adequately predicted at the current point in time. As in all relationship matters, the best contracts are between parties who honor and respect each other. Items that come up are resolved in a win-win situation between individuals who behave with integrity, dignity, and a willingness to understand the perspective of all parties involved. In these cases, the contract generally stays in the filing cabinet, and the parties communicate and work things out.

It's a small world. In this business, as in most fields, we will encounter the same players over and over. Especially now with the internet and social media, it is no longer possible to hide in another city or even another country to continue disreputable activities with a new set of targets. Small-time, petty swindlers will try to seize advantage and get one over on people, but they only get to do that once or twice at the most before their reputation is tarnished, and even the best persuasion skills they may have are easily invalidated by a quick Google search.

One personal example is "Chip", a property manager I hired a long time ago who stole $14,000 in security deposits. In the end, he was compelled to pay approximately $5,000 of that stolen money to the State of Colorado Real Estate Commission. This unsavory individual lost out on a lot of future business with me—and other people I could have referred him to. He actually ended up exiting the business after some disciplinary actions by the Real Estate Commission, including the public censure against his license that anyone with a smartphone could look up. Yes, $14,000 is a small windfall that pays a few deferred expenses, but losing one's livelihood over a small fraction of a year's pay and having to start over somewhere else, cannot be worth it.

Contrast that with a person who would have resolved the dispute that started out being about much less than $14,000, continued working as a property manager, and made many times the $14,000 over time.

Key Criteria for a Managing Partner of a Passive Real Estate Investment

"It takes someone with a vision of the possibilities to attain new levels of experience. Someone with the courage to live his dreams."

- Les Brown

"The problem with real estate is that it's local. You have to understand the local market."

- Robert Kiyosaki

Key Skills of a Managing Partner

A truly effective managing partner will be seasoned in all the aspects of putting together a team of investors, financing, closing, managing, and ultimately selling off a profitable real estate deal.

This skill set and experience should include:

•	**Ownership of other investment real estate**. This seems like a no-brainer, and it is critical. Only upon having owned other real estate and having made a few nail-biting mistakes on his or her own property can a managing partner have the experience to anticipate likely problems.

•	**Relationships with lenders** and a past history of financing investment real estate. Having a few loans with a positive payment history creates the same experience and proactive, risk-avoidant strategies also touched upon above. Lenders network as well, and having a history of successful past loan transactions, all having been paid on time, helps the next loan to be closed more effectively.

- **Good people skills.** This is an all-around must-have. Partners, lenders, local taxing and code enforcement authorities, tenants, property managers and the like must all be interacted with in a skillful manner which advances the best interests of the partnership.

- A **knowledge of the local market** where the property is to be acquired. There are lots of stories of out-of-town real estate investments that cannot be sufficiently evaluated, monitored and managed.

Donald Trump himself tells the story of having flown to Denver in the 1990s to evaluate a potential hotel acquisition that seemed exceedingly well priced, located right next to Denver's Stapleton airport. The team he was leading had decided to proceed with the acquisition and was having a drink at the bar before boarding a flight back to New York to handle the details and seal the deal. The bartender asked what they were in town for, and Donald told him they were looking to buy the hotel. The bartender asked, "What will you do when the airport moves in a few months?" As a matter of fact, Denver International Airport was set to open soon, and the Stapleton airport was to be shut down. This is now a residential neighborhood, and the hotels that remain are far from having the level of business (and valuation) that they would have if they had remained in direct proximity to an airport.

- **Property management experience.** Ample experience both performing property management and overseeing a professional property management firm is key to anticipating and addressing the challenges inherent to that function. For example, after my past experiences related to tenant security deposits, it feels risky trusting a firm with tens of thousands of tenant deposit funds, and I would rather have those funds in an account I have exclusive control over than that of some firm I may not have a longstanding relationship with.

- **Construction and rehab experience** in terms of upgrading and maintaining properties for maximum rental income and resale valuation. Management of contractors and construction efforts requires managing multiple dimensions. These include code compliance and proper building practices, interaction with local permitting authorities, management of contractors, choice of suitable and durable materials, and procuring the materials and contractors at an effective price. It also includes adhering to a tight timeline to allow remodels to be completed quickly in order to get the unit rented and cash flowing again as soon as practicable.

• **Experience in selling real estate for profitable returns**. There is a certain mental fortitude around selling high ticket items like real estate that must be mastered. A person who has sold multiple properties is more likely to have accomplished this. There is the art of patience, the art of negotiation, and the art of not turning down viable offers in the hope that a better one comes along.

A real estate mentor once told me that "The first viable offer is often the best one." Proving his point, my dad told me of a close friend of his who turned down a good offer for her house for sale, hoping for more money. She got no offers for two months, and then the property flooded due to a sewage backup while she was already living in her new home. This was a stinker of a surprise she only became aware of days after the damage occurred, which greatly compounded the harm. As is typical, sewage backup was not a covered risk under her insurance policy, so she spent $40,000 in repairs out-of-pocket. Ultimately, months later, she accepted an offer $20,000 less than the original offer she had turned down. Her unwillingness to seize the bird in the hand cost her time, energy, money and frustration.

With a cash flowing investment property there is less urgency of accepting an offer than that faced by the owner of a single family home who just got transferred out of state and is now making two mortgage payments. Yet timing is always a factor in making a real estate transaction successful.

Perhaps most important is not just how to sell, but when to sell. Waiting too long for the market to reach the zenith of its peak could prove challenging if there are any hiccups that delay the sale or if the buyer is unable to close. Selling too early can leave money on the table. This is especially true with a cash flowing building where there is a positive monthly or quarterly financial return, and thus no pressure to sell, at a time when a boom market cycle could create an additional 10, 20 or even 30% of appreciation through a strong rental market with strong rent growth. This is a trend Colorado has certainly seen from 2014 through 2018 as this is being written.

Competing with the Big Funds and Investors

In a passive real estate partnership, the syndicator (the person bringing the investors together), who is often (but not always) the active or managing partner, performs a lot of the key services, or oversees that they are performed satisfactorily. In doing so, the syndicator provides the mechanism for passive investment.

The syndicator does the work for the passive investors, and the assemblage of multiple investors creates economies of scale, allowing for purchases of bigger properties, where there is less competition, lower per-unit costs, and bigger potential returns. The syndicator also becomes a risk manager by potentially taking on personal responsibility as a guarantor on loans while passive investors' risk is limited to their cash investment.

Competing with the big funds and investors can be possible when the syndicator is able to turn around an offer in a day or two, while a fund might wait until their committee can review the deal and do all kinds of corporate style due diligence that takes days if not weeks while the nimble passive real estate partnership led by capable syndicator/managing partner already has the property tied up under contract for his group.

Tradeoffs in a Syndication

In a typical syndication, there are tradeoffs. A solo investor might be able to go "all in" and spend all their cash on acquiring an investment property, and "sail close to the wind" in terms of hoping that maintenance items will work themselves out until rent income allows for the accumulation of cash reserves.

I've done this when I started out, true to the maxim of putting all my eggs in one basket and then watching that basket very carefully. When I had a very small net worth, betting "the farm" was easy; there wasn't much at stake, and the returns were larger than the risk of loss. In my case, the risk was entirely individual. This is a strategy that is regularly seen in the marketplace for owner-operators. However, when working with others, and having a duty to preserve the investors' capital, I, and many syndicators, like to set up working capital reserves upfront (which is a highly recommended practice). The risk is not just the syndicator's; rather, we have multiple partners to answer to.

Prudence is generally the preferred course of action, rather than betting the farm, when other people's funds and the syndicator's reputation are at stake. The benefits are clear. However, there is an opportunity cost. Capital reserves don't earn returns the way actively invested funds do. This can lower the return on investment even though the necessary benefit is peace of mind and a contingency fund for any eventualities that might arise.

Key Personality Traits of a Managing Partner

Integrity

"To be successful in real estate, you must always and consistently put your clients' best interests first. When you do, your personal needs will be realized beyond your greatest expectations."

- Anthony Hitt, CEO of major real estate brokerage

"The best measure of a man's honesty isn't his income tax return. It's the zero adjust on his bathroom scale."

- Arthur C. Clarke

Integrity of course is pivotal to any partnership. An interesting way I got a concept of a prospective managing partner's relationship with money and sharing that money was in splitting a bill in a restaurant. A year ago I had dinner with an acquaintance who wanted to solicit me as a partner in a real estate deal he was putting together. When it came time to split the bill, he counted out change to get the food's pretax cost exactly right and he didn't seem to show an inclination to tip or even cover the taxes added onto the bill that weren't on the menu. To make sure the wait staff would give me good service when I came back to the restaurant next time, I paid for my meal at the menu price, as well as the taxes for both meals, and the tip for both our meals.

Yet, I was given a key awareness. Something about this prospective partner's relationship with money was off. He was looking for more than a hundred thousand dollars of investment from me, but in the same meeting he had me pay $5 of his share of the bill. Clearly, getting the better end of a deal, even when it's for a trifle as small as $5, was more important to him than the relationship with me and the waiter, both of which could have become repeat relationships. In researching this individual more thoroughly to confirm the objectionable feeling I got, I discovered that he had been sued by the Colorado attorney general and reached a settlement to pay $100,000 in fines. He had been running a locksmith scheme that duped and overcharged customers, typically doubling the initially stated fee once the service had been performed. This is an example of where a small transaction can create valid seeds of doubt that are worth following up on.

This is not to say that being extremely thrifty is always bad. I personally see an appropriate degree of thrift as good. However, people are more important than money. Being thrifty in such a way that one's partners don't receive the benefits of that thriftiness, as in the case of the unfairly split restaurant bill, is not desirable. I cheerfully absorbed the $5 that he ought to have paid, and that I paid to preserve the relationship with a waiter. If that was a matter of $500 or $5,000 or $50,000 in a partnership, I would not want to be in business with this person. Since this individual wasn't acting in integrity over $5, he was unlikely to get more honest as the amount of money—and the amount of temptation to be underhanded—increased.

Reputation

"Keep every promise you make and only make promises you can keep."

- Anthony Hitt

"All you have in business is your reputation—so it's very important that you keep your word."

- Richard Branson

Reputation is the foundation of any sound business relationship. As mentioned above, if you find documented verifiable facts about a person having been dishonest with others, it is only reasonable to assume they are likely to be dishonest with you. This includes checking for news stories, and with licensing organizations if they are in a profession that requires a license such as doctors, lawyers, real estate professionals, and so on.

Asking around also goes a long way. It's worth asking the individual for references. I interviewed one real estate lawyer who gave me a couple references. The references themselves, people she chose for me to interview, made me choose not to hire her. It's also worth asking around in the community if anybody knows the individual and has done any kind of transaction with him or her.

When a person is new in your town, you want to reach out on LinkedIn or similar social networking sites to find people from where this person moved from, who might give you a sense of what to expect in future dealings with this individual. Many times, people move for new opportunities in a geographic area. Sometimes, certain types of individuals might move because their reputation is tarnished in one location and they are looking for "fresh meat." It's worth being aware of that possibility and following the adage of "trust but verify."

Personality Fit

"Dig up all the information you can, then go with your instincts."

- Colin Powell

Personality is a huge part of being able to deal with a partner. There are somewhat conflicting dimensions to this. Having a person with a very different personality style can be tremendously valuable, as their strengths may offset your weakness and vice versa. Yet, interacting with people who are different from us can also be challenging, as it tests our flexibility and ability to deal with those who can be quite different.

In my own case I am challenged in interacting with people who are extremely indecisive. I have a hard time comprehending when somebody keeps needing more information on a matter where more information cannot guarantee a better decision, and often where more information is not readily available, or not even available at all.

At some point, if we are on the path to prosperity, we need to take risks and walk through a deep valley from which the destination is no longer within view. People who choose not to do that will never reach the promised land of abundance.

I have given extremely indecisive people who expressed interest in being my partners the benefit of the doubt. I then spent valuable time dealing with these commitment-averse people who diverted my energies from finding partners who were actually willing to make the move. In some cases this cost me precious days when I already had a property under contract and quickly needed to find a partner with the funds to consummate the closing, take possession of the asset, preserve the earnest money—and most importantly, to get on with the business of making money. Thinking about making money does not make money. Only taking action can get us there.

I love being in a business relationship with people who are positive and whose positive expectations attract positive results. This is just straight Law of Attraction. Any negative worldview that a partner (or any associate for that matter) has, can easily infect yours. Expecting negative outcomes can make them more likely to occur. As Tony Robbins says, "Get excited about what can go right, rather than fearful about what can go wrong."

Moreover, getting into the debate of whether a negative worldview is more realistic than a positive one can steal energy without providing value. It's worth evaluating strongly whether a seriously negative partner is the person you want to be engaged with in any business relationship that involves more than strictly minimal contact.

The best business partners are not the people you would just do that one partnership with, but those you could engage with in a long succession of partnerships. A poorly chosen business partner could easily deter you from further investments in that arena, and from finding that next high profit opportunity. Ideally, you want to partner with an inspiring and amazing individual, where your collective positive energy creates a synergy that generates results far beyond what either of you would have generated on your own.

Partnering with Friends

Partnering with friends can be extremely rewarding. You already know the individual. They may have the skills you both need to succeed. You like spending time with them and click with them at some meaningful level. At the same time, partnering with friends can create challenges. For one, being in business can threaten your friendship. You can easily go from being allies and friends to being individuals with misaligned goals, approaches and personalities. Your increased closeness and frequency of interaction could start to create conflict between you, rather than unity against outside forces.

My personal perspective is that becoming business partners with friends can force a very challenging re-adjustment phase, where you evaluate your relationship in a new light, and massively change the dynamics of your interactions. It's easy to accommodate a friend who can't quite pay their full half of the restaurant check at a monthly get together. It's different putting up with a friend and business partner who can't quite balance equitable splits in terms of effort, finances and assignment of credit for accomplishments on a daily basis. In a business partnership with a friend, you can quickly end up with what used to be a year's worth of inequity in the first 12 days of your business partnership. This will force you to move from a tolerant overlooking of infrequent imbalances to a real confrontation. Setting new boundaries and redrawing the lines of engagement takes work, a hard conversation, and a concrete renegotiation of respective roles, expectations, and interactions.

I have had successful partnerships bloom into beautiful friendships. I personally like the approach of forming partnerships with people where no renegotiation of existing roles and expectations is required. Nonetheless, with the right friend, a partnership can be a great way of having even more fun, and spending even more time with a good friend.

Red Flags to Watch out for with Potential Partners

Distractions in your colleagues' personal lives can detract from their full attention to the passive real estate partnership. Having a pregnant spouse (or being pregnant), or an ailing parent, or an ongoing divorce, or just having been named executor in an estate can all prove to be distractions in a business relationship. Limited partners can have spades of these types of issues going on and not have them interfere with the partnership. However, if the general partner has such issues, their focus on the partnership may temporarily become diluted.

Key Upfront Discussions with Partners

There are some key discussions to have with a potential partner early on in the relationship. Here's a set of valuable items:

How to Share Bad News

My first partnership ever, almost a decade ago, was a very run-down fourplex with a lot of deferred maintenance and some outright destruction by tenants. For example, overuse of Drano to clear clogged drains had all but destroyed much of the cast iron drain piping. Walls and ceilings needed to be opened up to replace the Swiss cheese of cast iron drains with black ABS "plastic" pipe. Likewise, the boiler piping was corroded badly with multiple leaks, and even many of the heavy, thick, seemingly indestructible cast iron radiators leaked.

The only prudent course of action was to tear open even more walls and ceilings and replace all those as well. And that wasn't the extent of it. There were more problems than I had anticipated, and my remodeling budget and contingency were low by about $7,000.

I was initially mortified at how best to share the bad news. I felt I had given my word about the budget and struggled with embarrassment at having mis-estimated. I debated covering the short fall myself and just skipping having the conversation. After much deliberation, I finally shared the bad news at a Vietnamese restaurant near the property. To my great relief, my partner fully understood. He appreciated how I had gone the extra mile to address the items that needed to be corrected to have smooth tenant interactions and virtually no maintenance for a long foreseeable time. In the end, the extra work led to a somewhat better quality of finish that translated into higher rents, such that the extra budget was recaptured. My lesson was to stop overthinking and just share things as they are when they come up. This path has stood me in very good stead.

Broaching the topic of how to deal with bad news early on creates more transparency in the partnership. It also establishes a communication pattern centered on a person's natural risk tolerance and ability to deal with divergences from a plan. This partner had started off as a Navy fighter pilot, and then moved on to becoming an airline captain. In his daily routine, divergences from plan occurred regularly, and they just needed to be handled. Long discussions about why they occurred were less of a factor than managing them to have a successful landing in the long run. We both shared the belief in doing some sort of debrief to capture learnings and optimize responses in case of future similar eventualities.

One thing to be aware of is that real estate goes up over time, but it may not always go up to the degree you want in the time horizon you want. If there is a period of time, most commonly at acquisition, when the rehab takes longer, such that there are additional costs longer, coupled with a slower time to getting rent cash flows, or possibly not as much rent appreciation as desired, that does not say anything about the true potential of a property. After a period of stabilization, a well-managed investment can easily become a long-term star property which spits out regular cash windfalls like a winning slot machine.

It is our human tendency to think in very short-term increments. That is also one of the reasons the stock market is often such a poor investment. To maximize quarterly and yearly returns, companies often do things that look good in the short run but are horrible in the long run. One of the most famous tales of this is the story of International Harvester (remember International trucks and tractors?), which one year declared record profits and massive executive payouts and bonuses, and just months later was on the brink of bankruptcy, ending with the sale of parts of the company and shut down of the rest.

While short-term setbacks do not affect the long term profitability and success potential of a property, they can however significantly affect short-term and possibly intermediate-term results. Some of this can be mitigated with adjusting costs elsewhere. My conviction as a professional in the property rehab and rental business is that there are different finish costs that I can apply, which can create different rent tiers. Often a bigger investment in the tenant finish may, from a short-term perspective, create the misperception of a lesser return. I fell into this trap early on in my landlording career, but have reconsidered over time. I have well over 500 tenant years of direct landlording experiences and have learned a more enlightened perspective.

There are a number of intangibles that I like to consider:

A better finish attracts a better quality of tenant. That quality tenant is more likely to take good care of a property, and to either stay longer, and/or to vacate the property in much better condition so that it can be re-rented faster, at a better rate, once again to a better quality of tenant. This is why for true results, a property should be held for a number of years, such that the initial investment can be recaptured, and such that the sale is timed to coincide with both having a seasoned building with multiple years of very positive operating numbers, and a great market cycle for selling investment property.

Underlying such a philosophy is my firm conviction about doing the right thing. There are no shortcuts to a bottom dollar investment that somehow garners top dollar returns. I saw a panel discussion with Matt Zimmer, the co-founder of Lyft. He made the point that doing the right thing for drivers empowers them and puts them in the frame of mind to do the right thing for passengers, which is in the long run the best thing for Lyft. The same applies to all businesses, whether it be real estate, transportation, hospitality or anything else where there are people from whom we desire money in exchange for a product or service.

Certainly there are major capitalists and investors who may not like the short-term implications of that approach. There are even enough who have still done well for themselves to continue the misguided notion that bad business leads to positive results (even as they left a trail of wreckage behind them). Yet, I fully agree with the co-founder of Lyft that in the long run his wealth will be maximized by his "golden rule" based approach of doing the right thing for all parties involved.

Consumers are sophisticated, and we can all see through the ploy when a business is trying to charge more for a product or service than the quality of that product and service merits. On the converse, providing great value has always served me dividends. I like associating with people who share my perspective. Trying to convince a want-to-be slumlord that being a luxury lord is preferable can turn into an ideological debate in which neither side prevails.

Rather than having a core philosophical mismatch become an ongoing sticking point in a partnership, it's preferable to acknowledge differences and either reach an intentional, defined compromise or to seek out a partner who has a better alignment and fit.

Philosophy around Proactive Capital Improvements

"Stingy pays twice."

- Russian proverb

Another area to have a sense for a partner's preferences and philosophy is around capital improvements. I once had a partner tell me about his mentor, whose philosophy was that a roof should only be fixed or replaced once it has started leaking. My personal philosophy is that being proactive and avoiding the tenant inconvenience of needing to make drywall repairs and possibly remediate mold is far more optimal and much more cost effective.

I can schedule the roofer or other tradesperson at a time when the contractor is a bit slower in his business. This makes him willing to give me a better deal on doing the roof, versus needing to do an emergency repair at a time when multiple other neglected properties in the neighborhood also need emergency repairs. Of course this "I've got eight roofs to fix before the next rain" is a typical situation when there is an exceptional rain or hail storm or other weather cataclysm that makes all the marginal, end-of-life roofs in an area fail. This is also where contractors make their biggest profits. Hearkening the warning of the Russian proverb "Economy is good, but stinginess is terrible," I try to pay only regular price, or a bit less.

Having such discussions about philosophies around capital investment and ongoing maintenance upfront will allow potential partners to understand each other's dominant approach, and to reach a shared agreement on how to handle items, well before they might become a source of conflict later in the partnership.

I personally believe in doing things with class. This applies whether in my role as managing partner or in my personal life. That also means doing things right the first time, and attracting the tenants and end-of-partnership buyers who are willing to pay that premium for being in an environment where the property speaks of class, elegance, care, proactive maintenance, and a concern for doing things properly.

Anyone who studies the economics of luxury brands knows that most of the profits in virtually any segment of the market are made by the luxury brands. There is tough competition in the bottom segment of the industry, with razor-thin margins. The profits are made by the brands that are more exclusive, don't always compete on price, and that care about doing things well, rather than merely cheaply. I like buying at bottom dollar, but then repositioning the property to play in that higher market segments.

Always Write Things Down

"If it isn't written down, it didn't happen."

- Tom Clancy

"Until the contract is signed, nothing is real."

- Glenn Danzig

Any discussion of substance is worth writing down.

A long time ago I heard that Joseph Stalin ascended to his top post of General Secretary of the Soviet Union on the basis of having been the designated note-taker during meetings that involved his predecessor, Vladimir Ilyich Lenin. This book is not about being manipulative. However, being the person who documents their version of an understanding can provide benefits to all parties. It doesn't have to be an elaborate affair to document the outcome of a conversation. It is completely adequate to use something as simple as an email saying "We discussed that we need to replace the roof on 123 Main Street. I will get three bids from different roofers, and we will review them together and then pick the best one. I aim to do that in the next 3 weeks. Please let me know if there's anything I missed."

Given an email like that, there can be no discussions later about a different recollection of the outcome of the meeting. I personally notice, over time, that what was discussed gets hazy in my recollection, and I know I'm not the only one. Having emails to quickly browse through is invaluable to jog everyone's memory and make sure the discussion and the viewpoints of all participants are fairly represented.

Ultimately, it is always easier to change an agreement down the road than to put one in place after the fact.

How to Succeed in a Partnership

One of the things I always find amazing about certain workplaces is that individuals of vastly different backgrounds work together, and enjoy working together, in a way that would have never happened without the existence of an organization that serves as a glue to bring these people together. Partnerships can be the same, providing not only investment opportunities and capital creation, but the creation of relationships between people. These can often be individuals who might not have sought each other out to spend time together socially, but whose business involvement creates a very beneficial and expansive partnership.

A passive real estate partnership is one of those instances where there is a strong benefit to diverse people coming together around a shared objective of profiting from a consolidated investment in substantial real estate holdings.

I believe that the number one criterion for succeeding in a business partnership is being committed to being personable. One way of doing so is to simply ask questions anytime there are points of view I might not have expected. Of course, it is easy to want everybody to be like me, which might make life a lot easier. However, we all know that is unrealistic, and even if it wasn't, it might become boring.

When there is a point of view expressed that differs from what I might have come up with, I often learn phenomenal things just by asking why that point of view exists. I have my own biases and gut reactions to events as well as my default "hammer" with which I pound down all the things that look like nails to me. There is power to realizing that my partner has a different version of the "hammer" with which they tend to pound anything that looks like nails to them. If we jointly evaluate the situation to see which default tool is a better match to the current circumstances, that is often extremely valuable.

Don't Sweat the Small Stuff

Whether it's the choice of what restaurant to have your business meeting at, whether it's a discussion of what the interior wall color should be, those things ultimately don't matter. What matters is that the business meeting happens and that the walls get painted. There is both action and movement forward, along with receiving market feedback, and being able to adjust course for the next series of actions.

The alternative is analysis paralysis. This is the state of staying inactive in the hope that an ideal, perfect solution might be found later. Long ago I fell in love with a paint color for interior walls, a light, cheerful color named "Orange Glow." A few tenants were *allergic* to the color and just hated it, choosing not to rent units painted that tint. Others were just fine with it. Over the course of time, I have changed my colors to a more neutral shade that doesn't create strong reactions either way. But in the end, having freshly painted units is still an advantage over some landlords, whose last paint job was done around Y2K.

On the converse, sweating the big stuff matters. This means finding an agreed upon path forward for any opportunity or challenge that needs to be resolved. This means having concretely defined goals. This means evaluating any contemplated decision against those goals to see if that decision helps us better meet those goals or detracts from meeting those goals. If there's divergence between the preferred decision and the previously defined goals, one of the two needs to change. We either reassess our goals or we modify the decision to be in line with the originally agreed-to goals. It is perfectly OK to adjust or even dramatically change an approach. However, such a change needs to be done with due consideration.

Communication is a core element of any successful partnership. Some people believe that shying away from difficult conversations is easier and safer. However, for me, having been in a variety of career roles centered around project and program management, where difficult conversations were inevitable, has given me a good amount of practice.

I have found that having difficult conversations can actually bring humans with different perspectives closer together. The core here is respect. By being willing to voice my perspective and listen to yours, I'm honoring your point of view. Having conversations about areas where we likely have a different perspective around solving an opportunity, allows our different perspectives to enhance the quality of the overall solution we define together. Most importantly, it is about respect of a partner who brings different perspectives, skills and life experiences to the table. Giving those partners the opportunities to share creates a benefit to the entire partnership.

Confronting Fear

"I learned that courage was not the absence of fear, but the triumph over it. The brave man is not he who does not feel afraid, but he who conquers that fear."

- Nelson Mandela

"Nothing in life is to be feared, it is only to be understood. Now is the time to understand more, so that we may fear less."

- Marie Curie

"Fear has its use, but cowardice has none."

- Mahatma Gandhi

One challenge I have found in this regard is dealing with individuals whose point of view is heavily colored by fear. Some people have been trained to fear loss, to fear that all tenants are less ethical and less able to live up to their commitments than other people, to fear the government, to fear losing all their money and being homeless... The list of potential fears goes on and on. Yet there are no new fears. In fact, most of the fearful thoughts are well-rehearsed loops that are repeated despite infrequent or illogical justifications for their existence.

Yes, fear is part of the human condition. On a bad day we can all ruminate on our fears and make that bad day worse through the quality of our thoughts. Many fears are things we have inherited from our parents' grandparents and beyond. Some of us still have ridiculous fears that may have reflected a gloomy perspective for an individual growing up during the Great Depression, but that are virtually baseless given current economic realities. Writing down such fears can allow for clear, rational analysis. I have found that many of my fears that can sometimes drive my behavior in negative ways are unfounded and invalid in today's climate.

If we just stay in our head and let our fears run rampant, the way a squirrel or raccoon does when they get trapped in a house, those fears can create a real mess. Being aware of fears and being willing to call our partners on such fear-based ruminations is critical. Once again, being in a good partnership is about embracing a level of authenticity and vulnerability where we can have honest discussions that go far beyond the investment matter at hand.

"As above, so below. As within, so without."

- Attributed to Hermes Trismegistus, ancient alchemist

The quality of our thoughts drives the quality of our actions. As business partners committed to our mutual success, we can help each other upgrade not merely the quality of our actions but also the quality of our thoughts. The most amazing partnerships are where we are individuals working together not just for a shared common goal, but where our work together empowers us all toward being more successful in other aspects of our lives, even well outside the scope of the partnership.

Plan Ahead

"If you're embarking around the world in a hot-air balloon, don't forget the toilet paper."

- Richard Branson

Planning ahead is crucial, and easier said than done. If we could know what was going to happen, we wouldn't have to plan; we would just be able to act. Hindsight is 20/20. Trying to guess and proactively deal with things we don't know are going to happen can create a particularly painful form of brain damage.

One way of planning ahead is to just get good insurance.

Another way of planning ahead is to escrow funds for the inevitable unplannable eventuality.

At one property I own with a partner, we are escrowing about 20% of our monthly profit to deal with eventualities. For a long time this seemed elective, and to be a sizable drain on our cash flows. Then we had a couple tenant move-outs in short succession. One tenant lived in his unit for about 3 or 4 years, and this individual had damaged enough items such that a partial remodel was necessary.

Ultimately, this is an unfortunate reality of the rental game. Every once in a while, we encounter a scenario like this. We can control most of the variables and only admit tenants with great credit and excellent references. However, in this case, his girlfriend had the great credit and excellent references, and when they broke up and she moved out, he stayed a few more years. The good news is that we had annually raised his rents, such that despite having been a long-term resident, he was paying market rents. Also, he had lived in the unit for two or three lease cycles, such that spending a larger amount of money at the end of three or four years is similar to having had a smaller amount of vacancy loss and repair expenses at the end of a one-year lease twice or thrice. The beauty of the escrow fund was that distributions to us, the partners, were not negatively impacted by having a somewhat larger outflow of cash to remodel his unit all at once.

Being a successful landlord requires having the equanimity to not see tenant move-outs, with a worse for wear unit, as a personal attack on ourselves or our profits, and for all partners to share that view. As with anything, all damage is fixable. With a great property, in a fast appreciating rental market, it was well worth fixing. As a partnership, we elected to invest money to fix up the unit to make it the best unit in the building. In doing so, we were able to raise the rent by $1800 a year. This means that there is a good payback on the remodel cost. Between the property value increase and the improved cash flow, there was a long-term positive benefit to something which in the short term could have been considered a setback.

The Positive Impact of Raised Rents

"Don't let negative and toxic people rent space in your head. Raise the rent and kick them out!"

- Robert Tew

In instances like this scenario above, it's worth knowing the impact increased rents have on property values. When a property is priced at 100 times monthly rent, or in a strong seller's market, 150 times monthly rent, an extra $150/month in rents can create an additional building value of $15,000 to $22,500 ($150 × 100 = $15,000; $150 × 150 = $22,500).

A cap rate variant on this concept is that at 8% cap rate, raising income by $1,800 a year ($150/month × 12 months) creates an increase in value of $22,500 ($1,800 / 0.08).

Note that these approaches create different valuations. The idea is not necessarily about pinpointing the exact increase in value, but about showing a significant increase in values from a small uptick in property cash flows.

Long-term tenants are often a great customer to have. They require very little management or hand-holding during their residency. However, sometimes, these same tenants end up leaving in disgust because they have run down their unit to the point where even they no longer feel comfortable living there.

Ultimately it's worth knowing that having several move out, clean and release cycles eliminated creates significant cash flow benefits. It certainly limits the inevitable loss of rents during the period between when the old tenant moves out, the unit is cleaned, touched up, shown and released, and the actual move-in of the new tenant. At worst, it's simply a shifting of spending. Cash savings today eventually need to be invested in unit rehab at a future time. It's the human condition to want to imagine that when the tenant leaves always happens to be the worst time to have a momentary dip in cash flows. However, if I can renew a tenant at a competitive market rate and avoid vacancy in the next month or two, I would rather defer any vacancy and unit make-ready expenses until next year.

I much prefer to take on an attitude of gratitude and remember all the benefits of having had a long term tenant, even in the rare instances where they seemingly cohabitated with swine, and to just go ahead and deal with the apartment make-ready in an optimal way. This allows me to re-rent at the higher end of current market rents. Generally, the rejuvenated and upgraded condition of the apartment after the remodel puts the rental unit into a higher class of market rents following the remodel.

An amazing best practice would be to know the details of every tenant's departure plan from every residency unit, so that contractor bids for a speedy remodel upon a tenant move-out are ready to be signed off so work can begin immediately. However, this is requires a crystal ball insight into planning that is not always achievable. Recently, I had a 43-year-old tenant die in his sleep. He paid on time, and I had no reason to see him moving for the upcoming future. He had been a resident for about four years at the time of his passing.

Copying a mentor, a very successful investor on a big scale, I'm realizing that at some level, I must embrace inefficiency. That means being willing to go out there and do what it takes now. The only alternative is to stay in analysis paralysis while trying to put together the most optimal sequence of steps and activities. Inevitably, analysis paralysis means that actually performing those actions is delayed and deferred.

Getting out there with a reasonably good plan and just doing things, even if they could have been done more efficiently in hindsight, seems to be the hallmark of those go-getters who are making the most money in the business. It's a twist on the old phrase, "When the going gets tough, the tough get going." Importantly, they do not sit in their office, figuring out just exactly how to be optimally tough.

Benefits of Partnerships

"I would rather earn 1% off a hundred people's efforts than 100% of my own efforts."

- John D. Rockefeller

"If you want to go somewhere, it is best to find someone who has already been there."

- Robert Kiyosaki

"If you want something you never had, you have to do something you've never done."

- Thomas Jefferson

"90% of all millionaires become so through owning real estate."

- Andrew Carnegie

"More money has been made in real estate than in all industrial investments combined."

- Andrew Carnegie

"There are no secrets to success: don't waste time looking for them. Success is the result of hard work, learning from failure, loyalty to those for whom you work, and persistence."

- Colin Powell

The Knowledge and Insider Knowledge of a Good Managing Partner

In some cases, the syndicator identifies an uncommon opportunity through an off market property that is made available for acquisition, providing added value over typical broker listed properties. This is the value add of a good managing partner who is actively scouring the market place.

Enhanced Networking

"A friendship founded on business is better than a business founded on friendship."

- John D. Rockefeller

Enhanced networking is another benefit of partnerships. This can include anything from meeting other potential business partners to have other profitable ventures with, to access to key people like anything from CPAs to roofers.

One of my partners from an ongoing partnership we've had for about eight years was new to real estate investing. Through partnering with me, he gained access to a great plumber, roofer, painter, and several other trades, building his own team of preferred contractors who remodel his units when tenants vacate. He was blessed to use this team to successfully build a portfolio of rental real estate he now owns and manages.

Knowledge Transfer

Through our association, my partner was also able to watch and emulate key skills so that he could begin figuring out how to evaluate, purchase and manage his own portfolio of rentals. Certainly it takes the right, very motivated business partner to be able to gain this kind of knowledge from participating in just one business partnership, as well as a sincere desire to learn. This partner had it, and he made that work for him. His partnership investment created multiple returns, in this case a significant one being financial. But the one I want to emphasize here is around learning, education, and access to people and resources that are beneficial outside of the scope of the partnership. This ultimately created a whole new income stream where my partner, a retired pharmacist, now owns a portfolio of properties providing him with semi-passive income.

Risk Sharing

Risk sharing is an old practice of creating an alliance of multiple people who pool their skills, expertise and networks to make the alliance successful. Risk sharing also limits the downside for any one partner if anything untoward were to happen. Like Warren Buffett, my governing philosophy is to never lose money. Passive real estate partnership risk sharing has the beneficial effect of creating access to investments that are larger than those that could be achieved by most partners on their own. Large investments have economies of scale, and these create the potential for greater returns in addition to the risk sharing benefit. Risk is distributed, rather than concentrated on any one person. Moreover, multiple partners reviewing and agreeing to a risk means that the additional layers of analysis provide an increased likelihood of the certainty of success.

Here's an example of a financial risk I took in the context of a partnership with shared risk, that I might not have taken on my own. It's not a big one, yet it's one that I wouldn't have sought out without having a partner to run it by, nor without having a partner willing to actually put up their portion of the investment money. In this case it was putting coin operated laundry in the basement of a fiveplex we co-own. Somehow I had a mental concept that five units was not sufficient to gain an adequate return on the investment in the coin operated machines, which are relatively pricey compared to standard laundry equipment. Reviewing this with my partner, he disagreed, and based on his estimations we both agreed to try it.

The returns were spectacular. We paid off the equipment in roughly seven months. After that, the laundry income was sheer profit. The profits from investing in coin laundry will never be life changing for me or my partner. Yet it's an example of gaining a small additional cash flow and a very sound return on investment beyond rental income and one that I might have passed on without my partner's willingness to engage.

Economies of Scale

Economies are a beautiful factor that is extremely difficult to achieve for a small investor, and they're built into the larger types of investments a typical passive real estate partnership will be buying and holding. Shared roof, shared heating system, shared parking areas, and shared property management all serve to create a lower per-unit cost than traditional single family or small multifamily housing. This creates lower construction, operating and maintenance costs, along with the ability to achieve similar gross returns to those higher cost single family assets, thereby netting a larger profit.

The Cost of Not Partnering

Several years ago I offered a high school friend the opportunity to partner on a fourplex, since I was running low on funds for doing deals by myself. He looked hard at the deal, but in the end his wife talked him into buying a new minivan, which ate heavily into the cash he would have invested in this property. As I write this about five years later, I just finished submitting the assessment appeal where the assessor sought to tax that property as if, over the course of five years, the property had appreciated 351%. This is simply property value appreciation, not counting the positive cash flows month after month that would have more than paid the monthly loan payment on a very nice minivan. What's more, that minivan would likely be on its final few payments right now, and my friend would now have had the opportunity to finance something far nicer with the monthly cash flows.

I love the story in one of the Robert Kiyosaki "Rich Dad" books, where in order to purchase a Porsche, he finds an investment property that will cash flow enough to pay the loan on the sports car. Five years later, the head-turning car is paid off, and the property has appreciated. Now, the question is what to buy next, and where to park the growing fleet of cool cars. That is the power of a passive real estate partnership.

Complementary Skills

"Surround yourself with people who take their work seriously, but not themselves."

- Colin Powell

SEC Rules

There is a large body of rules around the topic of passive real estate partnerships, and any kind of exhaustive treatment of these is outside the scope of this book, Further, I am not a lawyer and am not authorized to give legal advice.

Nonetheless, here is a brief summary around getting started in a passive real estate partnership. Soliciting partners in a meeting of strangers is against the law. Managing partners may share strategies around apartment investing in an educational or other non-investment seeking context. Upon having established relationships with people, generally in a subsequent meeting, one may ask them if they are interested in investing. Simply soliciting people that a managing partner does not know for investment is not compliant with SEC rules.

There are costs of compliance with SEC rules, as with any other governmental regulation. These are simply a cost of doing business and are part of the cost structure which the passive real estate partnership calculates into the costs that precede profit.

Staying in the Game: Rent Hikes and Taxes

"The key to wealth is translating numbers back into modified activity."

- Tony Robbins

Nuisance Raises

To have an optimally cash flowing property, "nuisance raises" are a must. These are small annual rent raises that train tenants that rent trends upwards, the way taxes and insurance rarely if ever go down. These nuisance raises create increases in cash flows year over year.

Many individual investors, once they get a steady tenant, neglect to have that "difficult" conversation about raising the rent every year. By the end of a six, seven, eight or nine-year tenancy, that tenant might be paying a rent that is $500 or more per month below market. I myself did this with my first rental property. My third tenant in that unit stayed for nine years. Their rent was the same the entire tenancy. While they paid off almost a third of my mortgage, I also realize that I left about $15,000-$20,000 on the table because of my reluctance to have indexed their rents to the normal rent inflation. I am past that early reluctance now. I am older, wiser, and have a family to feed. This is a business and I run it as such.

For income property like apartment buildings where the value is 100 or 150 times the monthly rent, that lack of annual nuisance raises can lower the value of the property by tens of thousands just for one unit being rented for less than market rents, in addition to the lost cash flows. See the prior section on "The Positive Impact of Raised Rents" for a more detailed treatment of this topic.

Default Raises in Leases

Some leasing agencies, and many commercial leases, have default rent increases stated in the lease, such that at the end of the lease term, the rent might increase by 3%. In Denver in 2015 and 2016, residential rents increased so much that 3% would simply not have been enough to mirror the market. This lease clause could have restricted the ability to have market rate increases reflecting the 10 to 15% increases that were commonplace. Rather than burying a formulaic rent increase in the fine print of the lease, I recommend having the rent raise conversation when the leases come up for renewal, based on the true facts that govern at the time, and raising the rents at the appropriate rate. Commercial leases are a different animal, since commercial leases can be extremely long-term. However, for a one or maximally two year residential lease, limiting future rent raises is counterproductive.

Inflated Assessor Tax Valuations Caused the 2008 Housing Crash

The real cause of the housing crash in 2008 is not what most people think it was. The media is rife with speculation and theories around the cause of the housing crash. We all know the oft-listed culprits:

- Liar loans
- Irresponsible bankers who made negative amortization loans, collecting loan commissions at loan signing, and government bailout funded payments later
- Desktop underwriting and drive by appraisals that didn't actually reflect fundamental risks associated with the property, the neighborhood, and its interior condition
- A sudden drop-off in lending that made houses difficult to sell and buy since buyers were locked out of the financing market by regulators who tightened reserve

requirements for the small banks that really fund main street home purchases across America for responsible borrowers who don't fit in the box created by the big banks.

●   Straw buyers and fraudulent transactions that created mortgages that weren't going to be and couldn't have been paid But the root cause is quite different and hasn't been discussed in the media much: runaway tax assessments using automated valuation models or extremely optimistic assessor appraisals to generate maximum property tax revenues for municipalities across the country.

I saw this trend here in Colorado. Basically what happened is a giant distortion of property values based on a limited set of fraudulent transactions that became the bellwether for assessing all other like properties to drive tax collection. There were a series of transactions in Denver where a church group got parishioners to sign for loans backed by bogus appraisals that created market comparables that were grossly inflated.

In one example I am familiar with, a five-unit rowhome complex was acquired for $250,000. The property was subdivided into five separate units and each unit (based on appraisals that I don't have access to but that must have been fraudulent with interior pictures taken from somewhere else) sold for $150,000 each. At the sale, each unit was financed at $120,000 (or higher) per unit.

My assessment on the true market value was $75,000 or less, based on the condition and improvements at the time when I purchased a number of these out of foreclosure. This means that for an investment of $250,000, these individuals received loans of $600,000 (5 x $120,000). What I noticed is that the assessor's mailed notices of valuation, the basis for tax revenue collection, used these fraudulent sales as comps for an enormous number of not even remotely similar units, even across town, way outside the neighborhoods generally considered valid for comparables, to generate maximum revenues. Essentially, in the drive for tax revenue, these far higher market comparables were used to justify higher tax values even on dissimilar properties far outside the normal geographical area that is typically considered for appraisals.

At the time, many banks had zero closing cost loans, and they thus had incentive to lower the costs of appraising properties by using automated means that relied heavily on recent sales data and assessor data. Suddenly, based on data like these, property values came close to doubling, and this caused the entire market to shoot upward in an unsustainably rapid fashion based on data where there was no factual basis for this sudden meteoric rise in values. Just a few cases of fraud with artificially inflated sales prices all of sudden caused a massive increase in assessed values across the market. Banks seeking lower closing costs used assessor data as impartial and accurate data when, in fact, it was not.

The lag in property tax basis periods (in Colorado, the two year period preceding June 30th of the year prior to when you actually pay tax) means that the costs of that fraud take significant time to get weeded out of the system. Moreover, unless someone actively reports obvious anomalies with a sales transaction, and the assessor investigates and is able to confirm the irregularities, there's no easy way to determine that the sale of property X at Y dollars wasn't a good faith sale.

To complicate matters, the assessor has rules about not using foreclosure sales prices as appraisal data. The prior inflated sale that resulted in a foreclosure is allowed to be used by the assessor, while the sale during the same statutory 2 year period, at the foreclosure price isn't even considered for valuation purposes. This is even when the foreclosure sale is for less than half of the assessed value and therefore provides real feedback that something isn't right

I was able to get the assessor to correct their data in the case of my row houses with a thorough walkthrough by a representative of the assessor's office. The assessor agreed that fraud clearly was involved, as the never remodeled state of the units obviously didn't warrant the public record sales price that had been financed at 80% by U.S. Bank in all five units. This is a big exception, and a rarity in the assessment process, and was driven by my desire to lower taxes on four identical units I owned in the same row house complex. Many property owners typically don't contest their taxes, figuring that if they are paying a little more, the money goes to good causes like schools.

One discovers that there are some real challenges with the assessment process, but it's just part of the dynamic of making money in real estate. Some assessors are much more fair, factual and honest than others. Ultimately, the total valuation of all property is multiplied by the mill levy to create the pool of money the county will have to spend that fiscal year. The mill levy is the number the assessed value of each property is multiplied by to create the actual amount of tax due for each property owner. The mill levy changes each year, while the assessed value of a property typically is reassessed and updated every other year. Being unwilling to use accurate assessment valuations simply creates distortions for the assessor and the entire real estate market. Assessed values are not the basis for the tax amount due, the mill levy is. Assessed values are simply a means of fairly or unfairly apportioning taxes to individual parcels of property. If John and Paul have similar properties, but the assessor decides John's property is worth more, John gets to pay a bigger portion of the city's budget than Paul.

Don't Be like the Montego Bay Resort Owner Who Spends His Time in New Jersey

I once stepped off the plane in sunny Montego Bay, Jamaica, and chatted with a gentleman as we waited to clear immigration. He owns a resort in Negril, Jamaica, and also owns several rental properties in New

Jersey. He was furious at the property taxation authorities, which makes sense, since New Jersey is the most expensive property tax state in the U.S.[19] The authorities were over-assessing his properties and seeking to collect taxes based on what my friend described as fictitious values to bolster their leaky treasury. This investor told me that he was suing the taxing authority and complained that he would have to cut short his stay in Jamaica to return to the Garden State of New Jersey to appear for a court hearing related to this taxation matter.

I asked my friend if his court costs were staying in line with the savings he would get if he won. He conceded that the matter had become personal and he was spending far more than the achievable savings in taxes over the next two years until the next reassessment cycle. That was just the financial aspect. My friend clearly wasn't living the dream taking parts of his wardrobe off to get through metal detectors in a New Jersey court house, rather than disrobing to get a nice tan on a sunny beach in Negril.

This story always reminds me to be business focused. Business is business. Letting business become personal and negatively impact my life is completely counterproductive. Making business personal contradicts any sound business advice any good businessman would ever give.

I, too, have similar stories. One assessor in the West Metro area of Denver also in my personal experience seemingly lacks the integrity to do fair appraisals and collect taxes proportionally to actual property values from property owners in his jurisdiction. Trying to contest this ended up with me against three county employees, a mix of attorneys and licensed appraisers who ultimately were better at representing their view to the state board of assessment appeals than I was at representing

---

[19] https://www.thebalance.com/best-and-worst-states-for-property-taxes-3193328, accessed November 26, 2017.

mine. Now, I just pay the taxes, charge the tenants, accept a slightly lower rate of return if the neighborhood doesn't support rent hikes equivalent to the tax increases, and move on.

Life is short, and I can spend it earning more money and looking for opportunities to be successful, rather than fighting over matters where the adversary is the government and where, despite rules prescribing fairness, the outcome, when fighting against a team of on staff system insiders with a reputation to defend, may not always be fair.

Appeal, Appeal, Appeal Your Property Taxes

"If I am not for myself, who will be for me? If not now, when?"

- Hillel

Taxing authorities are in business for one thing: to collect taxes. Here in Colorado, this is done by creating an automated valuation model that is a best-guess computerized representation of real world values. It's like an assessor's version of Zillow—optimistic, and often just beyond wrong. Yet, while looking at Zillow may be a nice boost to your mood, there's a very real price tag associated with the assessor's valuation. In Colorado, state law is that the assessor's valuation is based on the value over the past two year period, ending June 30th of the prior year (the basis period), yet based on the condition of the property in January of the current year. Thus, if I fixed up a property last December, the value is based on the remodeled value even though during the basis period, the property was not fixed up and was worth far less. This gives the assessor room to ignore the value I might have purchased a distressed property for, and to tax me on the fixed up value, even though the property was not actually fixed up yet during the basis period.

However, I have found that appealing property taxes does create some amount of return on the not inconsequential investment of time and energy. It requires pulling comps, and submitting some relatively detailed paperwork. There is usually an initial review and possibly re-determination of value, and if I don't like the results of that and feel I have comparable sales to justify a further tax reduction, I can appeal again and present my case a second time in front of a supposedly neutral independent, non-staff appraiser.

In reality, I find that the same appraisers get hired back year after year, and I wonder if they act in a manner designed to ensure that they continue to be asked back by the county that engages the appraiser. The second appeal results in a second review of the property tax valuation by this "independent" non-staff appraiser. This second appeal also frequently results in a flat-out denial of my case.

I can choose to appeal a final, third time in front of the state board of Assessment Appeals. This is usually a fairly high tension appeal, with the dishonest assessor sending multiple attorneys to flank the what I consider "dishonest" appraiser in justifying their version of the property tax value. The combined brain power of four salaried experts against me typically results in my not getting my case heard the way I believe it should.

The hearing is procedurally based, rather than fact based, and it is a challenge as a non-insider to prevail in this type of forum. Yet I do regularly make a run at it. I choose not to accept unfair treatment from my government, and I also set the tone that I may not be the best person to overcharge with egregious valuations. I believe in fairness and paying what is owed, but not more than my fair share. For high valuation apartment buildings, assessing carefully whether to appeal is very worthwhile.

In the end, it is my civic duty to stand up to unethical behavior in government. If I won't, who will? If I act in a way that perpetuates and entrenches bad behavior in government, I am not doing my part as a responsible citizen.

Maintenance

Select an Annual Improvement Budget

"So there's this guy named Murphy and he has this law. I hate him."

— Christy Trujillo

No property is perfect, and there is always a case to be made for keeping both the hidden mechanical elements and the cosmetic curb appeal elements in better than average shape to attract higher quality renters and gain better cash flows. A budget is a great way to plan improvements on an annual basis and create predictability around maintenance costs and upgrades, rather than feeling whiplashed as long-neglected elements fail on a schedule chosen personally by the author of Murphy's law.

A good analogy for this is car repairs. Adhering to the maintenance schedule in the manual creates costs that are relatively predictable, even if they may temporarily seem higher than driving until certain parts fail catastrophically. I see this with people who gamble with their cars. They may get years out of driving that car without fundamental maintenance being performed. Then, all of a sudden, they end up with a $2,500 repair that imposes an immediate, generally unbudgeted cost, the alternative of purchasing another used car, or being virtually stranded, perhaps right when the timing is least appropriate from both a financial and a mobility perspective. The example is the tenant who sprains his ankle on Sunday and has his transmission go out on Monday, on his way to a job interview that could have resulted in a promotion and a raise. That is not a great time for walking, bicycling, or public transit.

With property, deferred maintenance is not an approach leading to success, especially when it's avoidable. Tenants have legally binding and enforceable rights, which, in most if not all jurisdictions, include the legal right to working plumbing, heating, roofing and window systems. Not being able to provide those, and not having a plan for when they must be restored quickly, can create a litany of challenges.

Exiting a Partnership

"Look on every exit as being an entrance somewhere else."

- Tom Stoppard

With any investment we get into there needs to be a good exit strategy. Similar to a bank CD (certificate of deposit), the best strategy for a passive real estate partnership is to stick with the investment for its intended duration. However, there are occasionally circumstances that necessitate an early exit to recapture capital you need for an emergency.

Obviously when you ask a question of "When does the partnership plan to sell the property?" the managing partner should have a very good idea. Yet, allowing circumstances to dictate selling the property too quickly is a sure way to lose out on significant potential returns. Moreover, resorting to such a "desperate seller" approach shows a lack of maturity and a lack of the long-term focus on building true wealth on the part of the managing partner. For me, in the last two partnerships I have done, I structured the partnerships to agree on a five-year minimum hold. For one of those partnerships, we are now in year seven and have elected with a unanimous vote to continue with the partnership, due to better than predicted monthly returns that make selling the building uneconomic. We would not be able to gain similar monthly cash flows if we attempted to re-invest the sale proceeds with the investment opportunities we see available on the market right now.

On a different partnership, one of the partners wanted to exit, and the others wanted to remain. An appraisal was performed, determining the value of the building, and the partner was cashed out by me choosing to buy him out. Even though that partner needed to cash out because he had made some other investments for which he was needing additional capital, this former partner still says that his investment with me was the best real estate partnership, if not the best investment, he had ever made. I feel his pain; he made some good and some bad investments. In the end, he needed to liquidate his good investment to prevent a severe loss on a bad investment. This is not wealth building, this is battlefield triage, pure and simple. Yet. Having this real estate partnership that was a very successful one, gave him a fallback position he would not otherwise have had.

The easy, standard way to have the partnership exit and dissolution is when the property is ultimately sold and all of the partners receive any remaining portions of their initial investment back, as well as their portion of the gain from the sale of the property. How an exit from the partnership works is spelled out in the operating agreement or partnership agreement. A second way of exiting the partnership is to either have one of the other partners buy out the exiting partner, or to have the LLC buy out that departing partner. It is important to note that there is no instant liquidity in a real estate partnership. It is not like a mutual fund where you call your broker, and then as of 4 pm the next day you are liquidated out of your position and have your cash disbursed to you.

Real estate partnerships need some time to value your stake if there is a pre-sale distribution of your partnership interest. This valuation is needed to have either the LLC owning the partnership or one of the other partners buy you out. This should be relatively smooth, assuming you're looking to accept a sale at a value that is mutually agreed on by the parties. The typical time frame is one to three months depending on the property and the timing of all the parties involved, which may include appraisals.

General Guidelines on Cashing out of a Partnership

My recommendation is to cash out when the partnership is doing most well. Ideally, as with any investment, a long-term view of growing your money successfully is better than allowing a situation where you need to liquidate early. Regardless, external circumstances like divorce and other financial mishaps can happen, and these scenarios can be accommodated.

Check in with a manager of the partnership if there is an appetite from the partners or from the LLC that owns the partnership itself. The manager of the partnership should have a good pulse on the appetite of other partners to perhaps increase their investment in the partnership or for the LLC itself to take on your stake.

If there is a recent appraisal available, that is always helpful. Regardless, the managing partner should have an assessment of value. If you are in agreement with this, then that helps you assess the value of your stake of the partnership. If there is not a reasonable appraisal available, and you do not like the managing partner's opinion of the current value, you will need to procure an appraisal, which typically you will have to pay for yourself.

Cashing out this way is similar to any other real estate transaction. You set your price and wait for offers. If the partnership or one of the owners wants to buy, you will get an offer. When stating that the partnership wants to buy, this means that the partnership LLC purchases your stake using capital reserves or cash flows that the LLC has available, and the stake you sold now increases the ownership stake of each remaining member of the partnership in proportion to their ownership share. Once you get an offer from either the partnership or one of the other partners, you negotiate with them just like you would selling any other piece of real estate.

It only makes sense that you will price your partnership investment at its real value. Consequently, you should be able to sell it to the partnership or to a fellow partner within a couple of months. If you are not able to get a sale within that time, you consider adjusting your price lower. If neither the partnership, nor any other individual partner is interested in cashing you out, the managing partner should solicit an outside investor to join the partnership and purchase your share.

Typically a partnership agreement states that anytime a partner is looking to be bought out early, that the company and the other partners have a first right of refusal to buy out that partner. Only once those opportunities have been exhausted and there's no one interested, then the manager should support you in finding an outside investor to buy in by taking on your share.

I have not personally encountered a situation where an investor felt stuck and was not able to exit their share of the partnership. Indeed, with one of my partners who needed to inject funds into his bad investments, selling out of that partnership early created a more than 200% profit on his initial investment, not counting the positive monthly cash flows he received for approximately four years.

Growing Your Wealth

"Ideas can be life-changing. Sometimes all you need to open the door is just one more good idea."

- Jim Rohn

"The rich get richer."

- Unknown

The way I made it, through real estate, to being a self-employed entrepreneur with the freedom to "heal hurting houses" as my hobby—not to mention the freedom to travel, to write, to spend time with my son during the week, and to live a life I can be proud of—was to reinvest my real estate profits. The first few investments didn't throw off enough cash to rapidly grow the pot that I could invest in real estate, and so the early trajectory was slow, but it did gather steam as I added on more, and then another and another cash flowing property into the mix. My mantra was not to spend, but to save my real estate cash flows and have them available as the seed capital for my next real estate investment.

Once I owned about ten properties, and they all cash flowed well, the monthly sum of proceeds I was banking to buy the next good deal I came across started being meaningful. And that process kept reinforcing itself. I went from needing to wait a year to buy the next deal, to nine months, to six months, to being able to buy a property every three months or so. I consider myself blessed that early in my investing career, I was able to separate my costs of living from my investments. I was able to direct wage income toward my investments, and I did not need to tap into investment cash flows for my daily life. Without that, I would not have been able to build my real estate portfolio at the rate I did. It takes snow to make snowballs, and it takes money to make bigger sums of money. We all have money coming into our lives. What we do with those funds is what separates the winners from the destitute.

I read an interview with a destitute gambler once. He bragged that he often made $2,000 or more per day, much of it tax-free. But with a cocaine habit, reckless spending, and friends all holding their hands out, he never saved any money. Now he has nothing to show for his past successes. My heart bleeds that someone who once earned so much couldn't find a way to invest in something that would provide for him when he hit another losing streak. Whether it's a gambler, or the homeless guy who has found the corner where he makes $500 a day tax-free, many such individuals, who have found ways of earning money quickly, don't have the mentality to hold on to it or make it grow.

For me, real estate is that way of investing hard-earned cash so that going forward, my money is no longer hard-earned. Real estate is safe the way the stock market is set up not to be safe. Real estate provides regular monthly returns and inflation indexed cash flows without forcing me into crazy patterns of earning money. Ultimately, real estate also provides substantial equity appreciation that I can refinance out and invest in other properties, or that I can capture at the sale to be the down payment for my next bigger property.

About the Author

Fleming Schutrumpf is an accomplished real estate investor who started investing in real estate when he was 22 years old. Fleming has built houses, remodeled several dozens of units, and purchased more than $10 million worth of property for his portfolio and as part of partnerships he had engaged in.

Fleming prides himself on being a strategic thinker who is able to find and exploit contrarian opportunities in the marketplace. Fleming appreciates the art of taking undervalued properties with deferred maintenance and terrible curb appeal, and making them sought-after, shiny examples of what's possible in terms of revitalizing neighborhoods, providing eager tenants with great homes at prices that are fair to the tenants and profitable to the owners, and making formerly dilapidated properties cornerstones of a profitable investment portfolio.

Fleming enjoys masterminding with fellow high net worth investors who seek to grow their income and their wealth while providing a needed service in the community.